D0899765

# Inspiration for Songwriters
## Tips and Tricks to Unlocking the Muse

by
**Stan Swanson**

Stony Meadow Publishing
Denver, Colorado

Stony Meadow Publishing
Broomfield, Colorado

www.StonyMeadowPublishing.com

Inspiration for Songwriters
Tips and Tricks to Unlocking the Muse
Copyright 2006 Stan Swanson
All Rights Reserved
ISBN-13: 978-0-9787925-0-3
ISBN-10: 0-9787925-0-5


Printed in the United States of America

Without limiting the rights under copyright reserved above, no part of this publication may be reproduced, stored in or introduced into a retrieval system, or transmitted, in any form, or by any means (electronic, mechanical, photocopying, recording, or otherwise), without the prior written permission of both the copyright owner and the above publisher of this book.

PUBLISHER'S NOTE:
This publication is designed to provide accurate and authoritative information in regard to the subject matter covered. It is sold with the understanding that the publisher and the author are not engaged in rendering legal, accounting, or other professional service. If legal advice or other expert assistant is required, the service of a competent professional person should be sought.

## DEDICATION

This book is dedicated to the musicians and songwriters I have had the pleasure of meeting and/or sharing the stage with over the years. Each of you has enhanced my life in some way and enriched my songwriting experiences. There are too many of you to name individually, but you know who you are. I would also like to thank Kenn Amdahl, fellow author, musician, songwriter and longtime friend, for giving me some valuable suggestions for this work. And I especially want to thank my soul mate and my wife, Joy, for allowing me to spend so much my time with all of my other friends – the songs I have written and performed for many, many years.

# CONTENTS

## Old Friends

"Old friends, Old friends,

Sat on the park bench like bookends..."

(From *"Old Friends"* by Paul Simon)

Old friends. I guess that's the way I look at songs I've written over the years.

They are threads in the fabric of my memory that weave together a tapestry of my yesterdays. They are a myriad of colors splashed on the easel that is my life. They are a strange and crazy cast of characters to say the least.

Among them are those who think they are quite humorous fellows. They spit out their lines and beg you to laugh before retreating in embarrassment to a dark corner. Several are sad-eyed girls with wistful smiles. They sit with their raspberry lemonades and wonder why you never asked them to dance.

A blue-eyed blonde from Germany I knew decades past lounges on a bar stool by the stairs. I spoke little German and she spoke little English, but that was acceptable. We never did too much talking anyway. There were other ways to pass the time.

There are those who are quite boisterous, demanding to be heard. They love their rock and roll, but never quite forget their roots in the folk music of the sixties. There are others who meekly raise their heads to see if I notice they even exist. I wave to relieve their anxiety, but sad to say, there are some which have been forgotten forever.

I'd like to think that most of my friends gathered here tonight are good characters. Possibly even a majority of them if I give myself the benefit of the doubt. And trying to be as objective as possible, I'd like to think that more than a few are even great. But many of them, I fear, are only average at best. They are faces on the bus that you won't remember next week even if you traveled the same route day after day. But they remain my friends just the same. How could they not? I am their creator.

And, yes, I must admit that some of these companions are simply terrible. Oh, they try to be good, even average. But some are so dreadful that perhaps you might wonder why I don't have them do push ups or sit in the corner or say a dozen "hail marys". It isn't their fault they aren't winners like some of the others. The responsibility lies solely with me. Maybe that's why I can never completely abandon them.

The great ones and most of the good ones are the friends I hang around with most of the time. They are the ones that fight for position near the top of my song list. I hate to play favorites, but hey, these are the guys that are good enough to get me a gig once in awhile. (And heck, they love the spotlight and applause almost as much as I do.) They are so familiar I seldom have to refresh my memory of who they are or what they look like. I have memorized every line on each one of their faces. And when I take them out to that occasional gig, people seem to thoroughly enjoy their company and all feels right with the world.

But most of the time we all simply share space in the same small room. It's amazing that hundreds of us can live together in this dwelling we call home, but we do just fine, thank you. We make music here and there (although I must admit not quite as much as we used to). And new friends don't show up at the doorstep quite as often as they did once upon a time, but we're a happy group just the same.

But here tonight, in the quiet of my room, are the companions that have gathered and that hopefully I'll remember and visit for many years to come. For I know that without these old friends, my world would be a much emptier and sadder place.

"Old friends,
Memory brushes the same years,
Silently sharing the same fears.
Old friends..."

# How To Use, Misuse or Abuse This Book

There is really no correct way to use this book. It is filled with ideas to lure the muse out of hiding. It is littered with tips, tricks and information to invoke inspiration. Use it as you wish. I find it useful as a daily inspiration guide. Flip to any page and ponder one of the song titles or ideas provided.

Other than these first few pages, the book wasn't meant to be read in one or even several sittings. Use it as part of your complete songwriting experience. Think of it as part of your songwriting toolkit. It's main purpose is to serve as bait to lure the muse out of the closet, the attic, the garage or wherever she might be hiding. Curiosity might have killed the cat, but it's something inspiration can rarely ignore.

# Hang That Song in the Louvre!

"I'd like to go back to Paris someday
and visit the Louvre museum,
get a good running start,
and hurl myself at the wall..."
(From *"Ain't That Pretty At All"* by Warren Zevon)

Inspiration. That's what it all comes down to, doesn't it?

You are a songwriter. I am a songwriter. We are siblings with ink stains on our fingers and throbbing skulls from pounding our heads against the wall. We search for a swift and evasive muse that never seems to be around when we need her.

We write our words on napkins and envelopes and scraps of paper we find on the floor. We nourish and feed our words in the hope they will grow into creatures we can be proud of. We are part of a special breed of brothers and sisters that enjoy something few in the world share – the love of songwriting.

But what do we do when the Muse decides it's time to take a vacation to the Caribbean? We certainly can't afford to follow her. Our instinct is deep. We simply wait for her return and each time she leaves we fear that maybe this is the time she won't come back. Why should she? After all, who could resist the relaxation of the sand and surf of Martinique or Barbados provides?

I think that's the part that frightens us most. For we can no more stop writing songs than we can stop breathing. In fact, death may be the only thing that will eventually end the songwriting cycle for most of us. And so we breathe a deep sigh of relief when the Muse shows up on our doorstep at least one more time. It seems she had a return ticket after all.

But the question remains. Why does she disappear when we need her help the most? It's not like she has a 9 to 5 job. Where does she go and why? Is she hiding in our sock drawer? Is she on a flight to Paris? Are there ways to summon her back before she's finished contemplating the Mona Lisa and patting herself on the back for all the help she gave old Leonardo? Can we find that special lure that glitters at the end of our line and reel her in even when she resists?

The answer is yes, my friend, we can. She may be hiding in your coat pocket in the closet, but she's extremely inquisitive and there are ways to summon her out of hiding. You should also be aware of those times when she is near even if you weren't intending to sit down and write some music this day. She might be sitting next to you on the bus or walking next to you at the flea market. You never know when the opportunity for creativity might rise, so you should always be prepared.

## Fishing for Songs

Songwriting might be compared to fishing.

Some fish come easy. You catch your limit so fast you feel cheated, but you head home with a grin on your face and a soul full of satisfaction.

The easy ones come quick, but are satisfying just the same. You throw your line into the clear blue water and within seconds you feel the tug. There is barely a struggle as you reel the prize in and remove it from the hook. And you think, "wow, this is a piece of cake. Might as well be shooting fish in a barrel."

The easy songs are difficult to explain. They are so easy, in fact, you sometimes wonder where they came from. (Must have been lurking behind that picture of grandma on the dresser or something.) But maybe we shouldn't worry about where they come from. We should simply reel them in and feel proud of ourselves.

If only they were all so easy.

Others take an amazing amount of hard work before you finally reel them in. They swim lazily below the murky surface. My, god, you could almost reach out and grab one with your bare hands. But it all seems an illusion. They circle the hook, nibbling at the bait, but hardly ever bite.

We spend hours trying to catch them. We change baits and lures, but still can't seem to tempt the elusive creature. And when the thing bites, well, the ordeal has just begun.

You'd think the ones that are the hardest to haul in would be trophy catches – ready to mount above the fireplace in the den. They would be such marvelous prizes you'd have 8x10 photographs ready to share with everyone you meet. Sadly, that is rarely the case. The struggle or length of time it takes to write a song rarely has anything to do with its quality. A song that comes in minutes can be a darn good tune while the one you struggle with endlessly may amount to nothing more than an aging catfish that tastes like an old shoe.

I've written songs in minutes that were darn good tunes. I've also written "ten-minute" songs that ended up being nothing more than a mass of seaweed wrapped around an old boot.

The reverse remains true as well.

I have very good songs that took days, even weeks to write. And, unfortunately I've also spent weeks on songs that turned out to be barely salvageable. The one truth? Any song can be improved. Maybe you can't make a bad song great, but you can certainly make a bad song better.

But like that wise old fisherman, you have to keep throwing the line back into the water. If you give up too soon, you'll never know if that next cast might have hauled in the big one.

Patience doesn't pay off every single time, but the interest you collect in the interim is priceless.

## Unlocking the Muse

Where do songs come from? And do good songs and bad songs come from the same place? It doesn't seem logical, does it? But that's the way it works. Most songwriters have written many more "average" songs than good songs and probably more "throw-away" songs than great songs.

There is no magic formula for creating a good song every time you write. Even songwriting icons occasionally write a bad song. They simply don't record them for others to hear. (Well, maybe they've recorded a bad one here and there, but that's just my personal opinion.)

But if someone did create a perfect songwriting formula, it would also take away much of the magic that comes when that special tune pops its head up out of the ground now and then.

So, if you were expecting this book to provide a magical songwriting formula, I'm sorry. But what I do know is that most of the time it comes down to inspiration. It's finding the initial inspiration that is the stumbling block we usually face.

And while I don't have any magic formula, I do have lots of suggestions for making inspiration (and her good friend Muse) feel comfortable enough to sit down with you now and again even when she'd rather be somewhere else. Will the ideas in this book work each time you put them to use? Probably not. But if you simply use this book as one of the many tools in your songwriting toolkit, I guarantee it's a step in the right direction.

I wrote (or I should say co-wrote) my first song when I was thirteen or fourteen. I wrote a poem about some mundane subject like how beautiful the world was. (I think it was a project for English class.) My mother and grandmother thought it was wonderful, of course. But when my older brother took those words and set them to music, well... I felt something I had never felt before.

My brother had been playing guitar for a couple of years at the time, but the whole idea of learning to play guitar simply hadn't occurred to me. Hey, don't blame me. I was too busy attaching playing cards to the spokes of my bicycle. (Hey, it sounded just like a Harley! Well, almost...)

When I heard my poem set to music I was mesmerized. I was an instant convert and knew this highway called life had transformed into a 6-lane interstate thoroughfare. My grades took a dive, my mom occasionally complained about the racket and my fingers hurt so bad at times I wondered why I was torturing myself. I had never tackled anything with such determination and energy in my life. Heck, this was no box of Tinker Toys – this was magic!

I have probably written over 500 songs since that first tune co-authored with my brother. Many of them have been only average and yes, you will have to toss in a handful (or truckload) of poor songs. But when all is said and done, I believe I have also written many good songs. And I don't say that simply because my friends and family (and a few loyal fans) say so.

If you're a songwriter who has written for any length of time, you know when you've written a pretty good song. Have I written songs good enough to have made the charts if circumstances had been right? I certainly believe so and I think many of you would say the same thing with firm conviction.

Do I know what makes a good song good or a bad song bad? To a certain degree, yes. Most of us could sit down with a CD from an unknown singer/songwriter and pick out what we think are the best songs. They are the songs which, if you are a performing songwriter, are requested whenever you play a gig. Sometimes you might be surprised at the audience's choices, but for the most part, you know which songs they will enjoy time and time again.

When I was 14 or 15 I played my first gig at a junior high school talent show. I don't even remember if you had to audition. You probably just had to have enough guts to stand up there in the gym/auditorium and make a fool of yourself. And I did, of course. But what changed my music and songwriting forever was meeting another kid who had the same reverence for guitars, folk music and songwriting I did.

We played guitar, wrote songs and ditched school together for many years to come. It even became a competition of sorts. We wrote songs together, but we also wrote on our own and when got together we would share and compare our compositions. We spent many a day and night singing and sharing our music.

We have tales that were grand and as much a part of growing up as anything else during those years. We played at coffee houses (and baby showers) around the Denver metro area. We formed duets, trios, quartets and more.

We played folk music, jugband music and, yes, even some rock and roll. We were probably in the minority when we fell in love with the new Dylan after the Newport Folk Festival. We would have run out and bought electric guitars if we'd had any money to spend. We played "off-color" songs at school hootenannies and wondered if we'd get suspended. (We didn't. But we did get kicked out of school one year for having our hair too long!)

I spent many hours alone in my bedroom with the door closed. (Hey, I was practicing guitar and writing songs for goodness sakes.) For the most part I wasn't disturbed during the creative process. In fact, the only time I remember mom complaining was when I was writing a tune called "She's A Bad Woman". After hearing that line from behind my bedroom door forty or fifty times she finally told me to knock it off and play something different. Mom was somewhat of a religious woman and I think hearing about a bad woman from her teenage son in his bedroom was not comforting!

At some point along the way my music began gathering dust as time drifted on. (It has a nasty habit of doing that, you know.) My trusty old guitar was more of a conversation piece than anything else and looked pretty good hanging on the living room wall.

But a few years back something deep inside itched to get out. I dusted off the guitar and began writing again. (I even invested in a new set of guitar strings!) Now I don't know why I ever quit. I began playing gigs and enjoying them more than I ever remembered. I don't play out as much these days, but now I know I will never lay that guitar down for good and for that reason a new song will occasionally fill my living room. And that's all anyone can ask, isn't it?

## The Mystery of the Missing Muse

Whether you're new to the world of songwriting or you've been at it for years, you never fail to ask yourself the question. Where the heck does inspiration come from? What happens when I create a song and why is it easier at some times than others?

I know the same chords today that I knew yesterday and my vocabulary hasn't taken a drastic downturn, so how does it happen that sometimes when I sit down to write a song, well, I might as well be watching reruns of MacGyver. Why the heck does that happen?

Well, I'm really not too sure.

So if you are looking for some kind of magic you will be able to turn off and on after reading this book, well, I apologize. However, you can learn tricks that will lure inspiration out of its hiding place and those I can and will show you.

So who or what is the muse? Where did she come from? Why does she come and go so fleetingly? And why does she visit when I'm in the middle of something besides songwriting? It's not like I can tell the dentist to stop filling that cavity while I jot down the words to my next song. But there stands the muse, tugging at my shirt sleeve while the dental assistant sucks the spit out of my mouth with her magic machine.

The Muses, daughters of Zeus and Mnemosyne, were the goddesses of memory. They were believed to inspire all artists, especially poets, philosophers and musicians. Ah, now we're getting somewhere! They sat near the throne of Zeus and sang of his greatness, the origin of the world and the glorious deeds of great heroes. Now that must have been the life. Sounds better than playing for tips down at the local coffee house, doesn't it?

So, now that we know a little bit about the muse, how can we unlock it when we need it.? Well, that's why you paid your admission, isn't it?

## How To Write A Song

There are dozens of books available on "how to write a song" so I won't spend much time on the subject. (You will find a few of these titles listed in our resource section at the end of the book.) I will, however, provide a few basics for those who have never written a song and have no idea where to begin.

The best thing about songwriting is there is really no right or wrong way to do it. Unfortunately, this also makes the process more difficult to new songwriters. It's not the same process as learning a second language although the same commitment is certainly involved.

The first question new songwriters usually ask is "should I start with the lyrics or the melody?" It doesn't matter. As you advance in your songwriting skills, you will discover what works best for you. Some songwriters begin with the lyrics, some start with the melody and some create both at the same time. Many songwriters (including myself) do a mixture of all three.

If there is one songwriting rule, it is to simply write the song and get it finished. Don't stop to edit. Don't try making it perfect the first time through. Just write it. (I'm sure I will emphasize this more than once in this book, but that's how important I feel this "rule" is.)

The best way to do most things in life is simply do them. You've listened to music for years which means you already have much of the knowledge you need. You've probably also listened to the same type of music you'd like to write. But the best thing you can do at this stage is simply to listen some more. But this time listen to the song closely. Study the lyrics and the melody. Listen to a great song and ask yourself what makes this song stand out. Why do you like some songs and not others? These insights are the foundation for your own excursion into songwriting.

A good exercise for new songwriters is taking songs you like and "re-writing" them. Take the melody of an existing song and write new lyrics to it. Or take the lyrics of a song you like and write a new melody. This is a great starting point for new song-writers. Remember, this is simply an exercise. You never want to plagiarize another songwriter.

Just remember. Like anything in life that is worth accomplish-ing, songwriting takes time, patience and dedication.

## Other Stuff In The Book

### SONG TITLES

I've been jotting down ideas for original song titles as long as I can remember. I've written them down on the backs of deposit slips at the bank. I've scrawled them on the back of cash register receipts at the grocery store. I've jotted them down on napkins while I was waiting for my meal at the restaurant. And yes, I've even scribbled them on pieces of toilet paper in the... well, you get the picture.

They come when I least expect it. I'm sitting at a traffic light and up pops *"Waitin' For The Green Light And Running Out Of Patience"*. Or drinking a cup of coffee at the counter of a diner in a town barely big enough to have a name and a napkin becomes home to *"Secretly Saying Grace In A Greasy Spoon"*.

Anything you see can inspire a song title or the beginnings of an idea for a song. Maybe you're flying down the interstate when you notice an old backpack lying at the side of the road. Could such a small thing possibly inspire a song? Maybe. Ask yourself a question or two to help the story along. Who did the backpack be-long to? How did it come to be discarded along side the road?

Or let your mind take one of those gigantic leaps of imagination. Maybe you didn't find the backpack too inspiring. So change it to something else. A hitchhiker? A wilting sunflower? An old tin can? A dead gopher? Why not? Imagination has no laws, rules or regulations. That's the beauty of it.

So you think to yourself, why do so many gophers get hit by cars. You'd think they'd learn about those dangerous metal monsters over time. "Hey, Fred, don't run out there right now, don't you see that SUV barreling down... Oops." Or you wonder why mom and pop gopher didn't bring up their young ones a little better. And suddenly you have the ingredients for a song.

It's amazing where the mind can take you. You simply have to give it the freedom to do so. At times I'll simply sit in front of the television with notepad in hand and jot down song titles or ideas. Sometimes they come from something someone on that magic screen utters and sometimes it's a line coming out of nowhere.

I really don't care where song titles or ideas come from any more. I've stopped worrying about it and simply accept the muse as it comes. It's much easier that way.

So the 1001 song titles listed in this book have been collected over the years and interestingly enough, they were the inspiration for this book. Since that seed of an idea for a book was planted, *"Inspiration For Songwriters"* underwent many chameleon-like changes.

Several of the sections now appearing in the book were last minute additions. In fact, it seems as if each time I thought the book was finished, something new and exciting occurred to me and insisted on being included. (Sounds sort of like songwriting, doesn't it?)

In any event, I had literally hundreds and hundreds of song titles filling up desk drawers, plastic containers and old shoe boxes. I knew I would never use even a fraction of them and it seemed a waste to let them simply turn yellow with age and end up in a box of stuff my kids might find someday when I'm gone. Lucky for you (and me) song titles cannot be copyrighted. Do you really think there is only one song out there titled *"I Love You"* or *"Yesterday"*? So use them as you see fit. I think the odds of another songwriter picking the same title as you and having a successful song with it are highly in your favor.

## SONGWRITING TIPS

The songwriting tips included in this book cover everything from creating lyrics and melody to how to find inspiration when you're in a songwriting mood, but the old synapses aren't firing.

I wasn't sure I had enough information and tips to share, but once I started I knew my years of experience were enough of a catalyst to include plenty of ideas. It was at that point that I developed my "101" theory which stemmed from my 1001 song titles. If I included 10 song titles on a page I would have a book that was at least a hundred pages long. It was a good starting point. It also meant I could include such things as songwriting tips to fill those pages and add several more lists towards the end of the book.

It worked out well. Either the muse was with me at that point or Lady Luck had decided to pay me a rare visit that day.

You may agree with some of these tips and disagree with others and that's fine. I have found they all pretty much work for me as well as for many of my songwriting friends. Some ideas will work consistently and some might never work at all.

So use the songwriting tips as you will. I think you will find most of them helpful in some way. It is my intent and my hope that your songwriting is strengthened by the use of these tips.

## SOMETHING TO WRITE A SONG ABOUT

These ideas are simply suggestions you can use when you're in a musical mood, but nothing seems to be popping into your head to write about. Some of these ideas may be familiar subjects and others are a bit out there, but you've been provided a wide range of subjects to ponder.

These are suggestions you can use to fire up the old creative flame if you're sitting there with guitar in hand (or whatever instrument you use to create music with) but nothing seems to be working.

Simply turn to one of the suggestions included in the book and give it some thought.

Don't dismiss any idea that comes to mind. Close your eyes and really give it some thought. Does it remind you of a time in your own life? Does a line like "lying on your back looking up at the clouds" make you think about your youth? Does it make you think about a picnic a few years back with that someone special?

Read the suggestion and relate it to something personal. I think you will find this works much of the time. Even if you don't immediately write a song about the subject, make sure you jot the idea down in your notebook. You do have a notebook for your song titles and ideas, don't you? (The perfect companion to this book might be *"The Songwriter's Journal"* which is also available from Stony Meadow Publishing and most bookstores.)

Choosing one of the ideas every week (or each day if you're enthusiastic and don't have a "real" job) can be a great exercise. Try writing a song about the topic regardless of how you feel about it. Sometimes you have to force yourself. If your car has a dead battery, you need to jump start it, don't you? Well, the same thing applies here. Just try writing. The final results doesn't matter. It's the effort that counts. Nine times out of ten you will probably end up with a "throw-away", but it's that tenth time we all live for.

And don't dismiss an idea simply because you think the subject seems overly familiar. If a hundred different songwriters sat down and wrote a tune about visiting their grandparents, do you think we'd have a hundred songs that were the same?

## A WORD OR TWO TO INSPIRE YOUR NEXT SONG

This section serves more than one purpose.

First of all, like most things included in this book, these words are meant to inspire. Flip to any page at random, read one of the words and see if you can build a song around it. Maybe it will lead to a song title or maybe it will stimulate a memory of a certain time, place or person.

These words are also meant to show you how to use alliteration when creating titles or even complete lines in a song. Now some of the lines are pretty extreme and I wouldn't expect you to use them in a song, but they do show how a person can use alliteration to improve their songwriting. And besides, I enjoyed putting them together. Hey, it's my book, you know.

### A Word About Powers Words...

There are hundreds of words that are so strong they are able to almost instantly convey an idea for a song. I call these words "power words".

Power words convey strength and character. If power words were describing a person they would be words like radiant, robust, dashing, charming and charismatic.

Beautiful isn't a power word in my personal dictionary of definitions. Which sounds better: "she's beautiful" or "she's enchanting"? Enchanting is a much better word. So power words are the words that when you hear them you immediately imagine something extraordinary.

Magic, for example, is a power word. No doubt about it. Refrigerator is not.

Castle, crystal, heaven, hurricane, guillotine and vagabond are all power words. Lawnmower, microwave, garage, doorknob and pencil are not. See the difference? Now I'm not saying you couldn't write a song about a lawnmower or a pencil, but they certainly aren't power words.

The examples used in various parts of this book are, for the most part, power words. I hope this makes some sense and will help you use power words when writing your next song.

(Power words also make great names for bands, musical groups or titles for your next CD.)

Sit down with pen in hand and create your own word list. It doesn't matter if you're writing songs at the moment or not. Keep these words and ideas in your notebook. You never know when you might require a title or hook for a song you'll be creating weeks, months or even years from now.

## GREAT LINES FROM GREAT SONGS

It was an interesting project putting together these bits and pieces from great songs of the past few decades. It was fun going through lyrics and picking out lines I felt were extra special, but it was a lot more work than I imagined after searching through hundreds of song lyrics. You'll see what I mean when you read a few of these great lines.

The reason I included these lines was two-fold.

First, they are examples of great writing. Do not settle for second best when you are creating lyrics. Make them special. Make them words people will remember and they'll think about as they fall asleep at night.

The second reason I included these lines was to serve as inspiration. Sometimes all it takes is to hear a line from a song on the radio to make you want to grab your guitar or sit down at the piano and see what is ready to be splashed on the canvas we call music. After all, each and every song comes from inspiration of some kind. Use these great lines as tools to inspire you. Reflect on them and then create your own great lines for inclusion in your next song.

## AND THERE'S MORE...

At the end of our book you'll find several lists of things having the potential to inspire new songs. Each list is covered in more detail when you get that far.

"From Cavemen to Astronauts" gives you a list of 101 people you could write a song about while "Two Tickets to Timbuktu, Please" provides a list of 101 places around the world that could certainly inspire a song. "Give Me Liberty or At Least A Song So I Can Sing About It" lists 101 historical events just begging to be written about in song and "Lions and Tigers and Bears, Oh, My" provides a look at 101 citizens of the animal world that might inspire a tune.

"Planes, Trains and Automobiles" covers 101 modes of transportation that might inspire a song while "Mother Earth (For What It's Worth)" lists 101 flowers, trees and rock stuff. "Do Androids Dream of Electric Sheep?" covers the universe – literally – with

101 things from the world of outer space, astronomy, aliens, science fiction and fantasy.

"101 Songwriters You Should Listen to For Inspiration" lists some of the best songwriters to have graced the earth in the last few decades. You will recognize many of them depending on what type of music you usually listen to. These songwriters are not only meant to inspire, but are provided as a source of education as well. Listen to their songs. See how they write their music. See what they do that has made them stand out from the crowd.

Our list of "101 Albums/CDs You Should Listen to For Inspiration" offers some of the same ideas. Although many of the 101 songwriters listed above will also be included in this section, you will also find what we consider darn good music no matter how you look at it. These are some of the best collections of song ever recorded and belong in every serious songwriter's musical library. Put on one of these masterpieces and listen for a half an hour. You can't help but come away inspired.

And finally, "Play It Again, Sam" offers a list of 101 movies you should see the next time inspiration has left you alone staring at the living room wall.

Also included at the end of the book is our resource section which lists books, CD's, videos, software, recording equipment and all kinds of great stuff songwriters should have handy in case the muse should strike. This resource list is also available at our web site with links taking you right where you need to go should you want to order one of the items. (The web site address is http://www.Inspiration4Songwriters.net.)

Remember. There is really no correct way to use the rest of this book. Flip through the pages that follow when you are in need of some inspiration or need a good song title to start the muse flowing. Keep it handy and use it often. Let us know what you think of it and what you might like to see included in future editions. And I hope your next song makes you proud (and maybe a little money). But more importantly. Remember you are one of a special breed. You are a songwriter!

**SONG TITLES:**
1. **9.9**
2. **1929**
3. **2 Fast 4 U**
4. **4/4 Love**
5. **A Brand New Me**
6. **A Circle of Vultures Who Say They're My Friends**
7. **A Day In The Country With You**
8. **A Disney Kind of Love**
9. **A Half a Smile Away**
10. **A Hog's Life**

**SONGWRITING TIP #1:**

Here's your first tip. Try writing one new song each week for a year. It doesn't matter whether the song is good or not. Just write it! It also doesn't matter if the song is only 30 seconds long. Just write it! Make it a habit. Now this doesn't mean you're going to finish a song each time you sit down to write and even if you do it might not be a winner, but it's all part of the plan. Maybe you get a dozen good songs over that period. Maybe two dozen. Maybe three or four. But anyone who has written a really good song doesn't really remember the frustration or the pain that went into it. They simply know they have a song they can be proud of when all is said and done. Keep these bits and pieces in your notebook (as well as on tape) and review them occasionally. You might be surprised at how many of these bits and pieces eventually finish themselves.

**SOMETHING TO WRITE A SONG ABOUT:**

Your first kiss.

**A WORD OR TWO TO INSPIRE YOUR NEXT SONG:**

Senorita (Song For A Senorita)

**GREAT LINES FROM GREAT SONGS:**

"They paved paradise and put up a parking lot. With a pink hotel, a boutique and a swinging hot spot."
– Joni Mitchell (*Big Yellow Tax*)

## SONG TITLES:
11. **A Hundred Different Harbors**
12. **A Quick Trip to the Ceiling**
13. **A Thousand Years Will Come and Go**
14. **A Walk in the Park With My Baby**
15. **A Whole Lot of Me is Gone With You**
16. **Abandon All Hope**
17. **Aces and Eights**
18. **Adrenaline Rush**
19. **Aftershock**
20. **Again and Again and Again**

## SONGWRITING TIP #2:

Songwriters claiming they finished their last song in five minutes are probably stretching the truth a bit. Oh, I've written my share of five minute songs, but they usually weren't good. The secret is to take that five minute song and keep working on it. It's like finding an old lamp at the flea market. It doesn't take long to buy it and throw it in the trunk of the car. It's the work you do later with a little spit and polish that shines that sucker up into something magical. Make it your goal to take the time to improve your songs no matter how good you think they are. I've known folks who feel that once a song is finished it should be left alone. They say songwriting is a gift from the gods and you shouldn't mess with it. Hey, if you get a model airplane for Christmas it's probably a good idea to put the danged thing together and paint it at some point. Otherwise it wouldn't be much of a gift, would it? Don't be afraid to write and re-write. The change of a few words or notes can magically transform a good song into a great song.

## SOMETHING TO WRITE A SONG ABOUT:
Eating cotton candy at an amusement park.

## A WORD OR TWO TO INSPIRE YOUR NEXT SONG:
Locomotive (Locomotive Lullaby)

## GREAT LINES FROM GREAT SONGS:
"You know you're in trouble, when the bartender cries."
– Michael Peterson (*When The Bartender Cries*)

**SONG TITLES:**
21. **Ain't Me**
22. **Ain't No Fame, Ain't No Glory**
23. **Ain't No Love Like True Love**
24. **Air Pressure**
25. **Airgun**
26. **All Is Fair**
27. **Almost Not Crazy**
28. **Along the Timberline**
29. **Always Say You're Sorry (Never Say You're Wrong)**
30. **Am I Talking to a Brick Wall? (Oh, Sorry, I Guess I Am)**

**SONGWRITING TIP #3:**
There are some rhyming conventions that should be avoided if possible. One of these rhyming conventions is what we call "identities". (English majors might also know them as homonyms.) These are words that are spelled differently, but sound the same. Examples are "hair" and "hare" or "one" and "won". Because the words sound exactly the same, the 'rhymes' simply don't sound right. The solution? Don't use them. Another potential problem lurks in the form of near-rhymes. These are words like "same" and "train" or "love" and "rough". I rhyme the words "psychic" and "like it" in one of my songs and it works just fine, but you need to be careful. ("Should have read my horoscope, I should have been a psychic. Then I could see what's coming even though I might not like it." --*Some Things Never Change*) Near-rhymes are okay occasionally, but you should still limit how much you use them.

**SOMETHING TO WRITE A SONG ABOUT:**
Drinking a cold lemonade on a hot summer day.

**A WORD OR TWO TO INSPIRE YOUR NEXT SONG:**
Dawn (Dawn Dances With Dazzling Delight)

**GREAT LINES FROM GREAT SONGS:**
"Freedom's just another word for nothing left to lose. And nothing ain't worth nothing, but it's free."
–Kris Kristofferson (*Me And Bobby McGee*)

**SONG TITLES:**
31. **Amigo**
32. **An Ugly Kind of Love**
33. **Ancient Ties**
34. **And Every Step I Take I Trip and Fall**
35. **And Ice Cream on the Side**
36. **And Mama Said Goodnight**
37. **And Now The Love's Gone**
38. **And Some Nights I Don't Even Dream**
39. **And That's What Dreams Are Made Of**
40. **Angels Don't Drink Beer or Bourbon**

**SONGWRITING TIP #4:**

This may be one of the most important tips in this book. Diversify your music listening! It doesn't matter whether you write country music, contemporary folk or polka music. Listen to other stuff. If you write country music, listen to some hard rock. If you're a rock and roller, listen to some jazz. Do you want to write the same type of music over and over again? Well, if it's bringing you in an income, maybe so, but it doesn't hurts to broaden your horizon. Time spent behind the wheel of your car can be a great time to do this. Put it to good use. Hit the scan button and listen to what's playing on another station for a few minutes, then hit the button again. Hey, even Michelangelo would have appreciated the work of Norman Rockwell or Andy Warhol.

**SOMETHING TO WRITE A SONG ABOUT:**

How you felt on the first day of your last vacation.

**A WORD OR TWO TO INSPIRE YOUR NEXT SONG:**

Hurricane (Heart Like A Hurricane)

**GREAT LINES FROM GREAT SONGS:**

"The preacher said, you know you always have the Lord by your side. And I was so pleased to be informed of this that I ran twenty red-lights in his name."

– Mick Jagger/Keith Richards (*Far Away Eyes*)

**SONG TITLES:**
41. **Angels Follow Us Wherever We Go**
42. **Annexation**
43. **Another Night In Nantucket**
44. **Answers to Questions I Should Have Asked**
45. **Anthem**
46. **Apples, Oranges, Cookies and Cream**
47. **April May Turn Into June**
48. **Are My Arms Growing Colder?**
49. **Are You Brave Enough to Be a Coward?**
50. **Around and Around (And Upside Down)**

**SONGWRITING TIP #5:**

What inspires most songs? Feelings. They are born from longing, pain or desire. And these feelings are what you should focus on when you're stuck for motivation or searching for something to write about. Think about the mood you're in at that moment. Are you happy? Sad? Why? Are you falling in love? Out of love? Was work a real pain in the rear? Did you get stuck in traffic? Did some little old lady flip you off when you cut in front of her? Everything we do results in some kind of emotion. What this means is your next song idea is patiently waiting for you whether you realize it or not.

**SOMETHING TO WRITE A SONG ABOUT:**

Your first girl friend.

**A WORD OR TWO TO INSPIRE YOUR NEXT SONG:**

Victorian (Victorian Vanities)

**GREAT LINES FROM GREAT SONGS:**

"You don't tug on Superman's cape, you don't spit into the wind, you don't pull the mask off an old lone ranger and you don't mess around with Jim."
– Jim Croce (*You Don't Mess Around With Jim*)

**SONG TITLES:**
51. **As Far As the Road Can Take Me**
52. **Atmosfear**
53. **Baby  Got Me Goin'**
54. **Baby Can't You See It's Gone?**
55. **Baby Don't Know No Better**
56. **Baby Reads Me Like a Book**
57. **Back in Biloxi Again**
58. **Baby's Got the Blues**
59. **Back in the Groove Again**
60. **Backstage**

**SONGWRITING TIP #6:**
There are purists who don't believe in using a rhyming dictionary. It isn't cheating, my friend. Do you use a chord book to
learn how to play another variation of a Cmaj7th chord? Do you
use a thesaurus to look up a synonym? A rhyming dictionary is
like any other tool. Use it when you're stuck for a good rhyme,
but don't constantly rely on it. And although there are several
good rhyming dictionaries available, find one which was com-
piled specifically for songwriters. It will contain not only the
standard rhymes, but near-rhymes as well. I have three different
rhyming dictionaries on my desk and two software versions on
my computer. They don't get used a lot, but they are a godsend
when you really need it.

**SOMETHING TO WRITE A SONG ABOUT:**
The first time you flew in an airplane.

**A WORD OR TWO TO INSPIRE YOUR NEXT SONG:**
Peach (Probably Peaches, Possibly Pears, Perhaps Pineapple)

**GREAT LINES FROM GREAT SONGS:**
"You got to know when to hold them, know when to fold them,
know when to walk away, and know when to run."
– Kenny Rogers (*The Gambler*)

**SONG TITLES:**
61. **Backstreet Blues**
62. **Backstroke**
63. **Bad Guys Only Have Last Names**
64. **Ballad of a Love Lost**
65. **Ballad of the Brothers James**
66. **Ballad of the Dog**
67. **Ballyhoo For Me and You**
68. **Bandana**
69. **Bang Bang You're Gone**
70. **Bang, Boom and Bop**

**SONGWRITING TIP #7:**
Use song titles to come up with an idea for your next tune. (That's why I've included over a thousand in this book.) They are great little firestarters. A few words in a song title can convey a story whether it reminds you of something that happened in your past or simply conveys a new idea. A title like "Can't Buy Love at the Five and Dime" begs you to write the song. Keep a notebook and fill it with song titles. Add to it whenever you're in the mood or watching TV. Don't think about how you might create a song from the title. Just jot down titles as if you were making a list of songs on an imaginary CD or radio play list. I've written many a song simply based on a song title and I think you'll find it a useful tool as well.

**SOMETHING TO WRITE A SONG ABOUT:**
Standing barefoot in a cold mountain stream

**A WORD OR TWO TO INSPIRE YOUR NEXT SONG:**
Calico (Cozy Like Calico Kittens)

**GREAT LINES FROM GREAT SONGS:**
"Love when you can, cry when you have to, be who you must, that's a part of the plan. Await your arrival with simple survival, and one day we'll all understand."
– Dan Fogelberg (*Part Of The Plan*)

**SONG TITLES:**
71. **Banished to the Shadows of Your Love**
72. **Banjo Blues on an Old Guitar**
73. **Barefoot**
74. **Barnyard Blues**
75. **Beau**
76. **Beautiful Schemer**
77. **Been There, Done That**
78. **Been Thinking and Thought That I Would**
79. **Before We Saw a Beginning It Was Over**
80. **Beggar's Song**

**SONGWRITING TIP #8:**

A common mistake many songwriters make is starting a song strong (which is great), but finishing weakly. It's like we use up most of our creativity in the first third of the song and the chorus and then fail to live up to the standard we have set. Don't let this happen. Make your second verse as strong as your first and your last as strong as any previous verse. No, it isn't easy, but whoever said songwriting was a piece of cake? If it was we'd have fry cooks at McDonalds standing in line to trade in greased stained aprons for fame and fortune. Work on those last verses especially hard. Remember, those last few lines are the last lines your listeners will hear and recall. And because you finish your song with the chorus doesn't mean your last verse can be a throwaway.

**SOMETHING TO WRITE A SONG ABOUT:**

What it feels like to lie on a beach listening to the surf.

**A WORD OR TWO TO INSPIRE YOUR NEXT SONG:**

Bookworm (Bashful Bookworms Blink at Beautiful Blondes)

**GREAT LINES FROM GREAT SONGS:**

"I'd rather be a hammer than a nail."
– Paul Simon (*El Condor Pasa*)

**SONG TITLES:**
81. **Being Through With You**
82. **Bells and Bows and Painted Toes**
83. **Bells That Never Jingle**
84. **Belly Button Blues**
85. **Bet You Never Thought I'd Ever Leave**
86. **Better Think Before You Speak**
87. **Bidin' My Time**
88. **Big Ball of String**
89. **Black As A Cat in the Dead of Night**
90. **Blinded by the Starlight**

**SONGWRITING TIP #9:**

Explore your fantasies for inspiration. Now I'm not talking about those X-rated fantasies although you might not be able to tell if you listen to some of the lyrics out there today. What I'm actually talking about are the dreams and fantasies you have of walking on the beach in the Caribbean or trekking through the Amazon rain forest. We're talking about castles and dragons and angels and demons. If you can fantasize it, you can write it. It doesn't matter if you've never been there because you know what it feels like in your mind. It's your longing to swim in the crystal clear water off the Florida Keys that brings the muse out of her hiding place one more time.

**SOMETHING TO WRITE A SONG ABOUT:**

The smell of leather.

**A WORD OR TWO TO INSPIRE YOUR NEXT SONG:**

Earthquake (Even Earthquakes Evade Emotion)

**GREAT LINES FROM GREAT SONGS:**

"I wish I was in Tijuana, eating barbecued iguana."
– Stan Ridgway; Wall of Voodoo (*Mexican Radio*)

**SONG TITLES:**
91. **Blindside Love**
92. **Blonde Blue-Eyed Princess**
93. **Blood On My Hands**
94. **Bloop, Blip, Hug**
95. **Blue Tune**
96. **Blue-Eyed Girls**
97. **Blues Enough For Both of Us**
98. **Boiling Point**
99. **Boink!**
100. **Boston Knew Me Before I Was Blue**

**SONGWRITING TIP #10:**

Having trouble coming up with lyrics? You have a great melody going, but find the words aren't materializing? And we sure don't need another "When I woke up this morning" or "I'm writing this song about you" tune. Experiment with some free-form writing. Take out your pen and paper (you have them handy, don't you?) and simply begin jotting down any words that come to mind. Let your mind open into a stream of unconscious thought. (No, you don't require drugs or alcohol to do this.) Make sure you have some great nouns in there and then throw in a few verbs, adverbs and adjectives. Scatter them around the page and then take your pen and connect words that seem to belong together. You'd be surprised at what can come out of this simple exercise.

**SOMETHING TO WRITE A SONG ABOUT:**

Sitting in church through a long, boring sermon.

**A WORD OR TWO TO INSPIRE YOUR NEXT SONG:**

Derelicts (Do Derelicts Dream With Dignity?)

**GREAT LINES FROM GREAT SONGS:**

"I saw Satan laughing with delight the day the music died."
– Don McLean (*American Pie*)

## SONG TITLES:
101. **Bottle Full of Blues**
102. **Brand New Key**
103. **Bread on the Water**
104. **Bricks and Bones**
105. **Broken Dreams That Can Never Be Mended**
106. **Broken Ties**
107. **Brooklyn Tune**
108. **Building a Highway to Your Heart**
109. **Bugs on a Broken Windshield**
110. **Bums on the Boulevard**

## SONGWRITING TIP #11:
Keep a notebook handy at all times. And if nothing else, make sure you have pen and paper nearby. It doesn't matter whether you're at home, at work or in the car because you never know when the muse will smile and wink in your direction. And it never seems to fail that a great song title or a great line hits when you least expect it. You don't expect that 98-pound weakling on the beach to kick sand in your face, but you never know. And even though you think you'll remember that great line, most times you don't. Make sure you also keep a notepad next to the bed because I guarantee you seldom remember those great ideas that seep in when you're falling asleep or waking from a dream. You might also want to invest in a micro cassette recorder as trying to jot down ideas while in heavy traffic can be a bit dangerous.

## SOMETHING TO WRITE A SONG ABOUT:
Memories of your mother or father when you were a kid.

## A WORD OR TWO TO INSPIRE YOUR NEXT SONG:
Tumbleweed (Two Tumbleweeds Too Tangled to Tango)

## GREAT LINES FROM GREAT SONGS:
"Fool you once, you are forgiven. Fool you twice, you're just a fool."
– Mary Chapin Carpenter (*The Better To Dream Of You*)

**SONG TITLES:**
111. **Burning Up Daylight**
112. **But My Ship's Lost At Sea**
113. **But She Said A Cab Would Be Fine**
114. **But That's Another Story**
115. **Butterflies and Sweet Goodbyes**
116. **Calico in July**
117. **Call Me Bourgeois**
118. **Can't Buy Love At The Five And Dime**
119. **Can't You Feel the Power in Her Touch?**
120. **Can't You Send Her Home to Me Again?**

**SONGWRITING TIP #12:**

There seems to be an ongoing argument regarding whether songwriters should copyright their work. Those who don't copyright use the argument that any original work is your property as soon as it is created and lasts for approximately 70 years after your death. This standard applies to music as well as poems, short stories, books or anything else along the creative lines. The other side of the coin reveals the fact that while you did indeed write a song about brain-eating zombie Martians, you might not be able to prove it in a court of law. I recommend songwriters copyright their work if they are sending it out to singers, agents or publishers or if they perform their work in public. (Singing the song for relatives at grandma's house probably doesn't fall into this category.) Also remember: titles, names, slogans and phrases cannot be copyrighted.

**SOMETHING TO WRITE A SONG ABOUT:**

Sitting in a pub listening to good Irish music.

**A WORD OR TWO TO INSPIRE YOUR NEXT SONG:**

Glitter (Gold Glitters While Gamblers Grow Old)

**GREAT LINES FROM GREAT SONGS:**

"It's alright now, I learned my lesson well. You see, you can't please everyone, so you got to please yourself."
– Rick Nelson (*Garden Party*)

**SONG TITLES:**
121. **Can't You?**
122. **Caught in the Crossfire Again**
123. **Cereal Killer**
124. **Cerebellum Fire**
125. **Chances I'd Like to Take**
126. **Chances You Take**
127. **Chelsea Sunshine Morning**
128. **Chevrolet Lady**
129. **Chicago Doesn't Leave Here Anymore**
130. **Chicks**

**SONGWRITING TIP #13:**

Many songwriters don't share their creations. It's sad, but they do it for a variety of reasons. Maybe they feel they can't sing. Maybe they get stage fright. Or maybe they simply think they are writing for themselves and don't feel a need to share their music to feel fulfilled. Now I love to sing my songs even when I'm sitting around the house by myself. And yes, I enjoy hearing something I created whether anyone else is listening or not. But nothing compares to the feeling you get when you share your music with others. It doesn't matter if you don't sing well. People will be impressed you actually wrote the song. This is where your talent lies. Sing for your family. Sing for friends. Or sing for complete strangers. (Sometimes this is actually easier than singing for friends or family.) Find an open stage or a songwriter's circle. You will find nothing more satisfying than the applause you receive for one of your babies.

**SOMETHING TO WRITE A SONG ABOUT:**

Eating the best hot dog in the universe.

**A WORD OR TWO TO INSPIRE YOUR NEXT SONG:**

Ammunition (Angels Armed with Ammunition)

**GREAT LINES FROM GREAT SONGS:**

"Sometimes you're the windshield, sometimes you're the bug."
– Mark Knopfler (*The Bug*)

## SONG TITLES:
131. **Childhood Memories and More**
132. **Choo Choo's Blues**
133. **Chook-Chook-A-Looie**
134. **Chuggin' Along**
135. **Cincinnati Woman**
136. **Circles I've Drawn**
137. **Circus of Rainbows**
138. **City Eyes**
139. **City Streets, Country Roads**
140. **Clearing in a Yellow Wood**

## SONGWRITING TIP #14:
You don't have to know anything about music theory to be a good songwriter, but it doesn't hurt to know the basics. Sure, you can probably whip up a chocolate cake if you're good at following directions, but I'd wager a cake prepared by a master chef will look and taste a whole lot better. Now I'm not recommending you run off to the nearest community college and sign up for a music theory course although I won't discourage you from doing that either. But there are lots of good books on the subject and plenty of free information available online. Take advantage of these resources. I think you'll find your songwriting will improve with the more you know.

## SOMETHING TO WRITE A SONG ABOUT:
Riding a bicycle for the first time.

## A WORD OR TWO TO INSPIRE YOUR NEXT SONG:
Lace (Ladies In Linen and Lace)

## GREAT LINES FROM GREAT SONGS:
"You would think with all the genius and the brilliance of these times, we might find a higher purpose and a better use of mind."
– Jackson Browne (*Say It Isn't True*)

**SONG TITLES:**
141. **Close the Door (I'm Cold)**
142. **Close to Cryin'**
143. **Cold and Aching for You**
144. **Cold As Zero**
145. **Cold Touch of a Cold Wind**
146. **Cold, Cold Wind on a Cold, Cold Night**
147. **Colorado Breakdown**
148. **Comatose**
149. **Come Sit In My Camaro and Let's Be Cool**
150. **Come the Velvet Sun**

**SONGWRITING TIP #15:**

And what about our good buddy procrastination? I know we really don't consider him a good buddy, but he sure spends a lot of time hanging around my house. (Just ask my wife.) In case you didn't know it, procrastination and inspiration are mortal enemies. They really don't like each other much. (It was probably an argument concerning cleaning the bathroom or taking out the garbage.) Anyway, I guarantee inspiration will be nowhere in sight if procrastination remains by your side. So kick the fella out. Tell him the television is on the blink and you're out of nachos. Let him go hang out with some other songwriter across town for awhile. Once you do, it's much more likely inspiration will drop by for a visit. Oh, and forget the nachos. Offer her steak and lobster!

**SOMETHING TO WRITE A SONG ABOUT:**

You're a child afraid of monsters under the bed.

**A WORD OR TWO TO INSPIRE YOUR NEXT SONG:**

Bubblegum (The Best Bubblegum Blows the Biggest Bubbles)

**GREAT LINES FROM GREAT SONGS:**

"Every pleasures got an edge of pain, pay for your ticket and don't complain."
– Bob Dylan (*Silvio*)

## SONG TITLES:
151. **Come to Your Pappy Blues**
152. **Comes a Day for Dreaming**
153. **Common Law**
154. **Confetti Lover**
155. **Cool Blue**
156. **Corn Bread and Honey**
157. **Cornerstone**
158. **Cotton Candy**
159. **Could It Be Me?**
160. **Could It Be That You Don't Know Me?**

## SONGWRITING TIP #16:
Are you feeling, happy at the moment? Sad? Or perhaps you're feeling a bit depressed. After all, you checked the mail and all you got was a handful of bills and invitations to apply for 13 new credit cards! These are the perfect times to sit down and write. Put those feelings to use. Many a time I've written while depressed or sad or melancholy and find I not only get a song or two out of the process, but I'm suddenly much more cheerful than I was when I sat down. Of course, the opposite can happen when you're in a good mood, but if a good song is the trade off, it's usually worth it.

## SOMETHING TO WRITE A SONG ABOUT:
Sitting at a railroad crossing watching trains go by.

## A WORD OR TWO TO INSPIRE YOUR NEXT SONG:
Sermon (Salvation For Saints, Sermons For Sinners)

## GREAT LINES FROM GREAT SONGS:
"I said, baby, do you have no shame? She just looked at me, uncomprehendingly, like cows at a passing train."
– Don Henley (*If Dirt Were Dollars*)

**SONG TITLES:**
161. **Could You Ever Love a Geek?**
162. **Counter Clockwise**
163. **Cowboys Like Me**
164. **Crawlin' On Back to You**
165. **Crazy Ain't It?**
166. **Creation in E minor**
167. **Croissants and Coffee**
168. **Cross My Heart and Hope to Cry**
169. **Cruisin'**
170. **Crunchy Peanut Butter**

**SONGWRITING TIP #17:**

If you're trying to write a song evoking a certain mood, it doesn't hurt to try and recreate that mood. (Unless you're writing a song about the execution of a serial killer or a guy whose parachute doesn't open.) If you're writing a ballad, don't think the muse will flow freely if the kids are screaming in the background. Go down to the basement or out to the garage or even down to the park. Changing the location and scenery where you're writing can have a great effect on your music. Try writing a song in a completely dark room sometime and see what kind of "animal" emerges!

**SOMETHING TO WRITE A SONG ABOUT:**

Missing someone you loved who's gone forever.

**A WORD OR TWO TO INSPIRE YOUR NEXT SONG:**

Thunder (Thoughts of Thermonuclear Thunder)

**GREAT LINES FROM GREAT SONGS:**

"All lies and jest, still, a man hears what he wants to hear and disregards the rest."
– Paul Simon (*The Boxer*)

## SONG TITLES:
171. **Cry Like a Rock**
172. **Cry Like An Old Time Movie**
173. **Cryin' Like a Baby (And Reachin' For the Bottle)**
174. **Crying For Your Lover Is Like Barkin' at the Moon**
175. **Crystal Butterflies**
176. **Cute as a Button**
177. **Daddy Shot the Cuckoo Clock**
178. **Damsels in Disdress**
179. **Dance With Your Man**
180. **Dancin' to the Oldies**

## SONGWRITING TIP #18:

Want to be a better songwriter? Take music lessons. (And if you don't already play an instrument, take the time to learn.) I consider myself an above average guitarist. I'm no Stevie Ray Vaughan by any stretch of the imagination, but I can hold my own with many songwriters. For that reason, I never considered taking guitar lessons. Heck, I already knew how to play didn't I? But on the advice of a friend I decided to give it a try. It was a real eye opener. My guitar teacher turned me on to artists I had never heard of and I was suddenly learning new songs and found myself re-energized. It was also the first time I really learned there were such things as alternate tunings. This was an enlightening and rejuvenating discovery. In fact, what I consider one of my best songs was written in Open C tuning. I wouldn't have written the song if I hadn't taken those lessons.

## SOMETHING TO WRITE A SONG ABOUT:
Watching snow falling silently in a forest.

## A WORD OR TWO TO INSPIRE YOUR NEXT SONG:
Yesterday (Years and Years of Yesterdays)

## GREAT LINES FROM GREAT SONGS:
"There's an opera out on the turnpike, there's a ballet being fought out in the alley."
– Bruce Springsteen (*Jungleland*)

**SONG TITLES:**

181. **Dancing in the Dandelions**
182. **Dark Nights Find Me Howling at the Moon**
183. **Darker Than White**
184. **Dead Dog Blues**
185. **Deadland U.S.A.**
186. **Dead Sneaker at the Side of the Road**
187. **Dear Me, Golly Gee**
188. **December Dances**
189. **Deep In A Dungeon Inside My Cerebrum**
190. **Demons Die Without Salvation**

**SONGWRITING TIP #19:**

Inspiration and commitment don't necessarily write good songs every time out of the box. What we need sometimes is a little bit of luck and an occasional mistake or two. A mistake, you gasp?! That's right. It's the mistake you make in your chord progression that miraculously sound great. It's forgetting the words, but the words you make up on the spot are better than the original lines. Treasure these moments. When they happen, don't question them. They are a gift from the gods and you should simply accept them as such. Heck, you may find yourself making mistakes on purpose here and there. Hey, why not?

**SOMETHING TO WRITE A SONG ABOUT:**

Skinny dipping down at the pond.

**A WORD OR TWO TO INSPIRE YOUR NEXT SONG:**

Roulette (Ridiculous Reasons for Russian Roulette)

**GREAT LINES FROM GREAT SONGS:**

"You can't roller skate in a buffalo herd, but you can be happy if you've a mind to."
– Roger Miller (*You Can't Roller Skate In A Buffalo Herd*)

## SONG TITLES:

191. **Devil's Wearing His Sneakers So You'd Better Start Running**
192. **Destiny Never Did Me No Favors**
193. **Diamond Jim Came Strolling In**
194. **Dichotomy**
195. **Did Anyone See Saturday? (My God, Where Did It Go?)**
196. **Did Betty Boop Have A Belly Button?**
197. **Didn't I Know You in Denver?**
198. **Distant Love**
199. **Do Crickets Ever Sleep?**
200. **Do Elephants Ever Dance?**

## SONGWRITING TIP 20#:

If you write songs for a particular genre, then make sure this is where you get your constructive criticism. If you write children's songs don't expect to go down to the corner bar and get a valid reaction from the "happy hour" crowd when you play "Toot Toot Goes the Choo Choo". Or if you write a song on the depressing side, you probably shouldn't perform it down at the old folk's home. In other words, know your audience.

## SOMETHING TO WRITE A SONG ABOUT:

You're an innocent man on the night before his execution.

## A WORD OR TWO TO INSPIRE YOUR NEXT SONG:

Volcano (Volcanoes Void of Virgin Villagers)

## GREAT LINES FROM GREAT SONGS:

"Oz never did give anything to the Tin Man, that he didn't, didn't already have."

– Dewey Bunnell (*Tin Man*)

**SONG TITLES:**
201. **Do They Have Harleys in Heaven?**
202. **Do They Celebrate Holidays In Heaven?**
203. **Do Witches Really Fly? (And If So, Where's Your Broom?)**
204. **Do You Hear Romantic Music in the Middle of the Night?**
205. **Do You Think You Really Thought It Out?**
206. **Does Anyone Know God's First Name?**
207. **Does She Love It When the Music Plays?**
208. **Dost Thou Cry in Thyme to the Melody?**
209. **Dogtown**
210. **Doll You're Dressin' Fancy**

**SONGWRITING TIP #21:**
Most musicians know what a hook is and the purpose it serves. (A hook, by the way, is basically a catchy motif or refrain and many times is also the title of the song or a phrase repeated in the chorus of a song.) Do all songs need a hook? Well, if you're writing songs and would like to be commercially successful, the answer is yes. If you're a singer/songwriter who writes only to put original songs on your own CD or simply to play at your gigs, then it probably isn't as important. But remember, it's the hook that makes most songs memorable. You might have a nice little tune with some great words, but if there isn't a catchy hook that sends people on their way with something to remember, you don't have a commercial song.

**SOMETHING TO WRITE A SONG ABOUT:**
You're a Greek god looking down on the earth.

**A WORD OR TWO TO INSPIRE YOUR NEXT SONG:**
Halo (A Halo for a Hero)

**GREAT LINES FROM GREAT SONGS:**
"So often in time it happens, we all live our life in chains, and we never even know we have the key."
– Jack Tempchin and Robb Strandlund (*Already Gone*)

## SONG TITLES:

211. **Domination**
212. **Don't Be The Judge of Me**
213. **Don't Forget to Say You're Sorry**
214. **Don't Hit Me While I'm Down**
215. **Don't Know Why She's Crying (Was It Something That I Said?)**
216. **Don't Like It Much**
217. **Don't Make Me Laugh, I've Seen Your Girl**
218. **Don't Need No Blessings From the Pope**
219. **Don't Wake Me Up 'Cause I'm Still Dreaming**
220. **Don't You Think It's Funny, Honey?**

## SONGWRITING TIP #22:

Inspiration seems to come and go as she pleases. Hey, she has her own thing to do at times and can't be expected to sit in the corner all day long waiting for you to pick up your guitar or sit down at the piano. Sometimes you think you have control, but let's face it. She usually calls the shots. But I've found sometimes the best way to get inspired is to simply do nothing at all. Put the guitar away for awhile and do something else. Go for a walk. Mow the lawn. Lie down on the couch and take a siesta. At some point inspiration will feel ignored and insist you get on with things.

## SOMETHING TO WRITE A SONG ABOUT:

You're an eagle soaring through the evening sky.

## A WORD OR TWO TO INSPIRE YOUR NEXT SONG:

Alcoholic (Alcoholics Adlib Amazing Alibis)

## GREAT LINES FROM GREAT SONGS:

"Cinderella said to Snow White, how does love get so off course? All I wanted was a white knight with a good heart, soft touch, fast horse"
-- Chapman, Lerner and Roboff (The Kiss)

**SONG TITLES:**
221. **Down a Crooked Highway**
222. **Down in the Dumps Lookin' Up**
223. **Down in the Gutter Again**
224. **Dragonfly**
225. **Drastic Measures**
226. **Drive-In Passion**
227. **Drivin' Me Out of My Mind**
228. **Drivin' Towards Tomorrow**
229. **Drowning in Shallow Water**
230. **Drugstore Dice**

**SONGWRITING TIP #23:**

Once you have completed a song, let it sit for awhile. Let it age like a good bottle of wine. Well, maybe you don't want to wait a decade or two for the aging process, but you get the idea. I know it's hard to keep yourself from going back and fiddling with the melody and/or the lyrics, but if you let it sit for a day or two it will seem fresh and you'll find your re-write will come a little easier. You will also be able to look at it more objectively. If you insist on coming back to it several days in a row, make sure you come back and work on it even after you think it's done. I've changed words and tunes on songs I've been singing for years and most of the time it seems to make them a little stronger.

**SOMETHING TO WRITE A SONG ABOUT:**

Walking down a long dusty road on a hot afternoon.

**A WORD OR TWO TO INSPIRE YOUR NEXT SONG:**

Cheeseburger (Chubby Chicks and Chili Cheeseburgers)

**GREAT LINES FROM GREAT SONGS:**

"Then one day you find, ten years have got behind you. No one told you when to run, you missed the starting gun."
– Pink Floyd (*Time*)

## SONG TITLES:
231. **Druid**
232. **Drunk Like an Angel That's Fallen From Heaven**
233. **Dust in my Pocket, Dirt on my Shoes**
234. **Earthquake in Eden**
235. **Earthsong**
236. **Easy Chair**
237. **Easy Girl**
238. **Easy Kind of Love**
239. **Easy Street**
240. **Eat at Joe's (But Sleep at Josie's)**

## SONGWRITING TIP #24:
Can anyone write a song? Well, the answer isn't simple. Maybe anyone can write a song, but I don't believe everyone can write a good song and there are even less people who can create a great song. But writing a song is similar to writing a novel or painting a picture. It requires a streak of creativity. Now maybe you're creative and don't even know it. I know of little old ladies who didn't start painting until they were locked away in the nursing home who come up with some pretty cool stuff. That being said, I think most songwriters inherently know whether or not they have what it takes.

## SOMETHING TO WRITE A SONG ABOUT:
Seeing a snake in the grass out of the corner of your eye.

## A WORD OR TWO TO INSPIRE YOUR NEXT SONG:
Echoes (Eavesdropping Echoes)

## GREAT LINES FROM GREAT SONGS:
"You can't always get what you want, but if you try sometime you just might find, you get what you need."
– Jagger/Richards (*You Can't Always Get What You Want*)

**SONG TITLES:**
241. **Echoes**
242. **Electric Fantasies**
243. **Elevator Blues (I'm Up, I'm Down)**
244. **Eleventeen**
245. **Empty Alibis**
246. **Eskimo Love**
247. **Evangeline**
248. **Every Bunny Love a Rabbit**
249. **Every Time I Think I Know You**
250. **Everybody Dances**

**SONGWRITING TIP #25:**

So there you are sitting with guitar in hand or sitting in front of the piano trying to find a melody for your next song. You have some lyrics, but now you're searching for a new, exciting melody to go with them. But for some reason, it just isn't working. The truth is, it probably isn't going to happen that way. Most of us try too hard to get something completely different and this is understandable. But there are only so many notes in a scale. Step back and take another look. Try going back to basics and test a few simple chord progressions. Don't get fancy. Forget about augmented 7th diminished to the 3rd degree chords. How about C-F-G-F or C-Am-F-G? It's amazing how sometimes the simplest things can unlock something new.

**SOMETHING TO WRITE A SONG ABOUT:**

The first time you ever drove a car.

**A WORD OR TWO TO INSPIRE YOUR NEXT SONG:**

Devil (The Devil Dances When Daylight Dies)

**GREAT LINES FROM GREAT SONGS:**

"Time is an ocean, but it ends at the shore."
– Bob Dylan (*Oh Sister*)

## SONG TITLES:

251. **Everybody's Gonna Rock and Roll Tonight**
252. **Everyone Might Hate Me (But Honey I'm Still Breathin')**
253. **Everything I Once Held Sacred**
254. **Evil Like Love**
255. **Exactly the Way You Want It**
256. **Except When Cotton Would**
257. **Eye Candy**
258. **Fable**
259. **Fahrenheit**
260. **Fairy Tale Talkin' Blues**

## SONGWRITING TIP #26:

I use to think I would be able to write better songs if I simply had better equipment. After all, surely my songwriting would improve if I purchased that $2000 Taylor guitar I saw in the music store window. Right? Or if only I could invest in a fancy digital recorder. That's the way I use to think when I was writing novels and short stories. Surely my writing would improve if I had a new Dell desktop computer with a nifty flat screen monitor sitting on my desk, wouldn't it? Oh, I got my new Dell and I love it, but still end up writing most of my first drafts with a pen and a legal pad. The only way to improve your songwriting is to keep working at it.

## SOMETHING TO WRITE A SONG ABOUT:

Standing by a river watching the water flow by.

## A WORD OR TWO TO INSPIRE YOUR NEXT SONG:

Heaven (Hoping for Heaven, but Headed for Hell)

## GREAT LINES FROM GREAT SONGS:

"Day destroys the night, night divides the day. Tried to run, tried to hide, break on through to the other side."
– The Doors (*Break On Through*)

## SONG TITLES:

261. **Fake You Out**
262. **Falling Through the Cracks**
263. **Fancy Hats**
264. **Fandango**
265. **Far Side of Nowhere**
266. **Fault Lines of my Mind**
267. **Fear of Love**
268. **Feet As Cold As Ice and Snow**
269. **Ferris Wheel**
270. **Fifteenth Century Prayer**

## SONGWRITING TIP #27:

Stuck there on the sofa waiting for inspiration to strike? Well, you might have a long wait. She's probably out helping another songwriter who lives across town. But here's a thought. Try changing your character. Write from a different perspective. Look at a certain situation through the eyes of another person. Write about something that happened to your spouse or significant other as if you were seeing it from their perspective. Or simply change your personality completely. If you're shy most of the time, become aggressive and outgoing. Sometimes it doesn't take much to bring inspiration back into the fold.

## SOMETHING TO WRITE A SONG ABOUT:

Watching the ants stealing crumbs at a picnic.

## A WORD OR TWO TO INSPIRE YOUR NEXT SONG:

Lipstick (Lipstick Leads to Little Lies)

## GREAT LINES FROM GREAT SONGS:

"It's the heart afraid of breaking that never learns to dance. It's the dream afraid of waking that never takes the chance."
– Amanda McBroom (*The Rose*)

## SONG TITLES:
271. **Fighting With Myself (And Losing the Battle)**
272. **Fingers on a Blackboard**
273. **Firestorm**
274. **Flash of the Gun**
275. **Fleas**
276. **Flight**
277. **Floatin' at the Three Point Line**
278. **Floors Made of Wood**
279. **Flowers for Penelope**
280. **Fly Girl**

## SONGWRITING TIP #28:
Take the time now and then to go back and work on some of your older songs. I know I've said this before, but it bears repeating: songs are seldom truly finished. I went to a Dylan concert a few years ago and was amazed at how different some of his numbers were from the recorded versions. And if Dylan (maybe the best songwriter ever to grace this earth) does it, you know it can't be wrong. Take a song apart and examine it closely. Do this with your great songs as well as your not-so-great songs. You can make a good song great and an average song better with a little work. And don't throw away songs you feel don't live up to their (or your) potential. You never know when a "throw-away" song could turn into something special. You simply need to work at it and have lots of patience.

## SOMETHING TO WRITE A SONG ABOUT:
The stale smoke of an old cigar.

## A WORD OR TWO TO INSPIRE YOUR NEXT SONG:
Cowboy (Calloused Cowboys Curse Carelessly)

## GREAT LINES FROM GREAT SONGS:
"Nothing ever goes as planned, it's a hell of a notion. Even pharaohs turn to sand, like a drop in the ocean."
– Dennis DeYoung of Styx (*Nothing Ever Goes As Planned*)

**SONG TITLES:**
281. **Flyin' Down to Monterey On A Sunny Afternoon**
282. **Flying in the Face of Fear**
283. **For a Dollar and a Dime**
284. **For the Love of Laughter**
285. **For You**
286. **Forever's Almost Over**
287. **Four Fingers**
288. **Fractures**
289. **Freaks**
290. **Freckled Face**

**SONGWRITING TIP #29:**
Don't be a perfectionist, but strive to be a perfectionist. Okay, let me make some sense of that. Don't be a perfectionist when you are creating a new song. Just write. It doesn't matter at this point whether the words make sense or the melody is too simple or too complicated. Just get started. The objective here is to write the song. If you spend too much time writing the first two lines over and over because you think you can do better you may never finish. Writing the basic song should be your only concern. Then you can strive to be the perfectionist. (Or as close as we're ever going to come.) Even when I listen to classics I can see where a change of one or two words might have slightly improved the song. But you have to write the song in the first place. If you don't have a song, you have nothing to improve. So force yourself to write any way. If the words aren't coming, then hum the tune. If the melody isn't clicking, work on the lyrics. It may not come together overnight and may take weeks or even months, but eventually the song will be a "keeper".

**SOMETHING TO WRITE A SONG ABOUT:**
Watching an earth worm in freshly dug soil.

**A WORD OR TWO TO INSPIRE YOUR NEXT SONG:**
Wicked (Walk Wide by Wicked Women)

**GREAT LINES FROM GREAT SONGS:**
"Something's lost, but something's gained, in living everyday."
– Joni Mitchell (*Both Sides Now*)

## SONG TITLES:
291. **Free Like Fire**
292. **Freedom From the Chains**
293. **Freedom Street**
294. **Freeze Me**
295. **Frequent Flyer**
296. **Friendly as a Snake**
297. **Friendly Overtures**
298. **Frogs**
299. **From the Flames of the Inferno**
300. **Frying Pan Blues**

## SONGWRITING TIP #30:
You might be a great poet and think words will make your song absolutely fantastic, but the truth is most of the time the melody gets a song its initial attention. Song lyrics are like a car's engine while the melody is that sleek, fire-red fiberglass body with streaks of flame painted down the side. Now ultimately people are going to notice the car has a pretty powerful engine, but not before noticing what a terrific looking vehicle it is. Make your melodies stand out so people will get the opportunity to listen to the lyrics before all is said and done. Lyrics might make a good song a great song, but the melody will really make your song stand out. It should be familiar, yet catchy. This is what makes the process so difficult at times.

## SOMETHING TO WRITE A SONG ABOUT:
Being stung by a bee or hornet when you were a kid.

## A WORD OR TWO TO INSPIRE YOUR NEXT SONG:
Hillbilly (Hillbilly Hand-Me-Downs)

## GREAT LINES FROM GREAT SONGS:
"The best thing you've ever done for me is to help me take my life less seriously. It's only life after all."
– Amy Saliers of the Indigo Girls (*Closer To Fine*)

**SONG TITLES:**
301. **Full Tank**
302. **Galileo In Disguise**
303. **Gamble Your Love On Me**
304. **Garage Love**
305. **Gemini**
306. **Ghost at the Door**
307. **Giggles and Grins**
308. **Gimme the Bad News First 'Cause the Good News Doesn't Matter**
309. **Gimmie Gimmie Gimmie**
310. **Girl On Fire**

**SONGWRITING TIP #31:**
Whatever happens in the verses of a song should not bypass the chorus or vice versa. Remember, your song is a story and if your chorus gives away the "punch line" of the song before the last verse, then there's nothing left to the imagination of the listener. So tell your story in chronological order. Go back to your finished songs and make sure you have done this. Read your lyrics and see if you can find a timeline and that the order of your chorus, verses and bridge don't fall out of sequence. And if you ever re-write the words to one of your song's verses or the chorus, make sure the story stays in the right order and still makes sense.

**SOMETHING TO WRITE A SONG ABOUT:**
Driving down Route 66.

**A WORD OR TWO TO INSPIRE YOUR NEXT SONG:**
Blue (Big Bullies Bring Black And Blue Bruises)

**GREAT LINES FROM GREAT SONGS:**
"Young men flirt, at least they try, but pretty girls don't blink an eye. We hold on tight, but still we slip away. And the tide rolls a little closer every day."
– Stan Swanson (*Time Is The Tide*)

**SONG TITLES:**
311. **Girl You Gotta Catch My Mind**
312. **Give Me Back My Death Said the Resurrected**
313. **Give Me Boom Boom**
314. **Glances in Church**
315. **Glass Shoe Blues**
316. **God's On The Phone (Should I Put Him On Hold?)**
317. **Goofy Things I Wish I'd Never Said**
318. **Goin' Down In Flames**
319. **Going, Going, Gone, Gone, Gone**
320. **Gonna Be A Star**

**SONGWRITING TIP #32:**

So you're in a great relationship and you've written all you can about your current love. So what do you write about now? Why not drift back to your past? Think back to the time you began writing songs or playing guitar. What was it like? Who were your favorite artists at the time? I know whenever I feel stuck I go back to my roots and put on some Dylan or Donovan. Listening to those songs brings back memories of where I was at the time and what I was doing. And suddenly I'm fired up again and ready to go.

**SOMETHING TO WRITE A SONG ABOUT:**

The touch of satin sheets.

**A WORD OR TWO TO INSPIRE YOUR NEXT SONG:**

Dungeon (Damp Dungeons Demand Darkness)

**GREAT LINES FROM GREAT SONGS:**

"His eyes were two slits that would make a snake proud."
– Bob Dylan (Angelina)

**SONG TITLES:**
321. **Gonna Catch My Dream When I Wake Up**
322. **Gonna Have My Cake and Eat It Too**
323. **Gonna Leave You This Time (And It Ain't No Bluff)**
324. **Gonna Rock-A-Bye My Baby**
325. **Gonna Steal Your Love**
326. **Good Gosh, By Golly**
327. **Goody Goody Two Shoes**
328. **Gordon and Petty, Unser and Andretti**
329. **Got Nothin' But Time to Kill**
330. **Got That Volcano Feeling**

**SONGWRITING TIP #33:**
Meditation can be a powerful tool for songwriters. If you already know how to meditate, then use it to your advantage. And no, meditation isn't simply picturing some creature of the opposite sex walking through the room although this could actually work now that I give it some thought. I'm talking about real good old down-to-earth meditation. (Interesting, but before I fixed the typo, the sentence read "medication". Hmmm...) If you don't know how to meditate take a few classes or read a good book on the subject. It's a great tool each songwriter should have in their toolkit.

**SOMETHING TO WRITE A SONG ABOUT:**
What it must have been like to have been a cowboy.

**A WORD OR TWO TO INSPIRE YOUR NEXT SONG:**
Sunflower (Sunflowers Soaking Up The Sun)

**GREAT LINES FROM GREAT SONGS:**
"A little bird told me that jumping is easy and the falling is fun, right up until you hit sidewalk shivering and stunned."
– Ani Difranco (Swan Dive)

## SONG TITLES:
331. **Got You and Heaven Too**
332. **Gotta Be a Lie**
333. **Gotta Love You Babe**
334. **Gotta Sit Down 'Cause I'm Tired of Walkin'**
335. **Grandfather's Clock**
336. **Graveyard Blues**
337. **Gravity Moves Me**
338. **Greasy Spoon**
339. **Greenbacks**
340. **Gunslinger**

## SONGWRITING TIP #34:
It's a good idea to make the pitch of your chorus higher than the melody of the verse. This makes your verses recognizable as the meat and the potatoes of your song and the chorus the highly anticipated dessert. Take a look at most of the popular songs or songs you like. You will notice this happens much of the time. It is usually an instinctive thing, but if you find this doesn't ring true in any of your tunes, it might be time to do a little re-tooling. Also, when the melody of your chorus is in your highest comfortable range, it gives you room to make the verse lower.

## SOMETHING TO WRITE A SONG ABOUT:
Trying to talk a friend out of committing suicide.

## A WORD OR TWO TO INSPIRE YOUR NEXT SONG:
Vagabond (Vampires, Vixens, Vagrants and Vagabonds)

## GREAT LINES FROM GREAT SONGS:
"And I'm wondering where the lions are."
– Bruce Coburn (*Wondering Where The Lions Are*)

## SONG TITLES:
341. **Had a Strange Dream**
342. **Hanging By My Toes**
343. **Happenstance**
344. **Happy as a Horseshoe**
345. **Happy as a Hound Dog With a T-Bone Steak**
346. **Happy Socks**
347. **Has Anybody Seen My Hat?**
348. **Hate to Say I Love You**
349. **Hava Tequila**
350. **Headin' Eastbound in a Westbound Lane**

## SONGWRITING TIP #35:
What happens when you're sailing along and suddenly get stuck on a line you think is great, but you can't seem to make it rhyme without it feeling forced. Well, you can certainly turn to your favorite rhyming dictionary, but sometimes the best course of action is to simply leave the line and come back to it later. Once again, it's finishing the song that counts. And don't simply discard what seems to be a great line out of frustration. Nine times out of ten you'll find you can come back later and the perfect rhyme comes out of nowhere. Or try rearranging the words in the line so the end rhyme is different. And remember, it isn't necessary to finish a song in a single sitting. In fact, it seldom happens.

## SOMETHING TO WRITE A SONG ABOUT:
Driving down a dark street in the bad part of town.

## A WORD OR TWO TO INSPIRE YOUR NEXT SONG:
Laugh (Lucky Lovers Laughing)

## GREAT LINES FROM GREAT SONGS:
"In a dog's brain a constant buzz of low level static, one sniff at the hydrant and the answer is automatic."
– Lee, Lifeson and Pert of Rush (*Dog Years*)

## SONG TITLES:
351. **Headline News**
352. **Heaven Holds the Heart**
353. **Heaven Knows (But Just Ain't Tellin')**
354. **Heaven's Just Around the Corner**
355. **Heaven's On The Other Side of Town**
356. **Hello Red, Goodbye Blues**
357. **Here Comes That Same Old Feeling**
358. **Here's Hoping for the Best**
359. **Heroes and Sidekicks**
360. **He's a Lucky Dog**

## SONGWRITING TIP #36:

Don't be afraid to accept criticism of your song. Most criticism is offered with sincerity so don't feel like people are attacking you or your music. (Drunks down at the corner bar don't count.) And it's way too easy to find people who will tell you how good your songs are. They'll even tell you your not-so-good songs are great. But when a stranger tells you how much he likes one of your songs, you know you have something special. Constructive criticism can be your best friend if you allow it. Songwriter critique groups are great for this. Sure you'll hear some stuff you don't like and even suggestions missing the mark. But remember, you have the choice to ignore what you don't feel is relevant and use what are good, solid suggestions. And if someone tells you the melody to your latest creation sounds like Jack Johnson's latest release, you would do well to check and see if it actually does. Jack probably has a lot more money than you to pay lawyers.

## SOMETHING TO WRITE A SONG ABOUT:
The smell of a familiar perfume.

## A WORD OR TWO TO INSPIRE YOUR NEXT SONG:
Wheels (The Wheels Whisper Where)

## GREAT LINES FROM GREAT SONGS:
"It's like forty five horses running through the graveyard in yellow panties."
– Beck (*Cold Ass Fashion*)

**SONG TITLES:**

361. **Hippopotamus Dance**
362. **Hit Me Again 'Cause I'm Still Standing**
363. **Hold High the Shield**
364. **Hollow**
365. **Hollow Days**
366. **Holy Holy Holy**
367. **Honey Do You Want to Be My Long Lost Friend?**
368. **Honey, Hang Onto Your Hat**
369. **Honey, Your Halo Is Tilting Again**
370. **Hook, Line and Stinker**

**SONGWRITING TIP #37:**

You might be surprised at how many song ideas you can come up with by simply flipping through the morning paper or glancing at magazine headlines while standing in line at the grocery store. (Don't forget to have pen and paper handy.) Newspapers and magazines are great resources for songwriters for they give us ideas we probably wouldn't have thought of on our own. I mean, what songwriter would ever think to write about Elvis living on Mars and cloning little Elvi so they can invade earth someday if it hadn't been on the front page of The Enquirer? And if any of you think you might have come up with that idea on your own, I'd sure like to see what you keep in your medicine cabinet.

**SOMETHING TO WRITE A SONG ABOUT:**

A baby crying in the middle of the movie.

**A WORD OR TWO TO INSPIRE YOUR NEXT SONG:**

Chameleon (Chameleons Camouflage Colorlessly)

**GREAT LINES FROM GREAT SONGS:**

"There's ten stuffed heads in my trophy room right now, two game wardens, seven hunters, and a cow."
– Tom Lehrer (*The Hunting Song*)

## SONG TITLES:

371. **Hot Rod Rumba**
372. **How Did You Know I'd Been Crying?**
373. **How I Love Your Laughter In The Morning**
374. **How Much Will You Give Me For This Dime?**
375. **Hubba Hubba**
376. **Hubcap Annie**
377. **Hula Hoops and Hopscotch**
378. **Hymn for Her**
379. **I Ain't Afraid of Much (But She Sure Scares Me)**
380. **I Came Across a Fairy Tale (And It Was You)**

## SONGWRITING TIP #38:

Your title and the first few lines of your song should give you a clue where the song is headed. Let the words guide you. If your song title is "Love Never Knows When It's Leaving" then you should probably be writing a slow ballad. If the title is "Throw Me, Sock Me, Roll Me, Rock Me", then your song should probably be up tempo. Of course, there are exceptions and sometimes the results can be startling. "I Love You" sounds like a ballad, but can't you also picture a heavy metal band screaming out "I Love You!" on stage? Let common sense guide you, but don't become its slave.

## SOMETHING TO WRITE A SONG ABOUT:

You need to make an urgent phone call, but your cell phone's dead.

## A WORD OR TWO TO INSPIRE YOUR NEXT SONG:

Spider (Spooky Spiders Spinning Spirals)

## GREAT LINES FROM GREAT SONGS:

"Bubba shot the jukebox last night, said it played a sad song and it made him cry."
– Dennis Linde (*Bubba Shot The Juke Box*)

**SONG TITLES:**
   381. **I Can Hear You Whisper, But It Sounds Just Like a Scream**
   382. **I Can Talk to Cats and Dogs (But I Can't Talk to You)**
   383. **I Can't Count to Twenty, But I Know That You're the One**
   384. **I Christen Thee Love**
   385. **I Could If You Could**
   386. **I Gave A Flower to the World**
   387. **I Got the 4-Speed Blues**
   388. **I Got Two Left Feet But I Still Feel Like Dancing**
   389. **I Just Can't Feel That Way Again**
   390. **I Just Don't Think It Matters**

**SONGWRITING TIP #39:**
So what happens when you sit down to write your next song, but the words you put to paper don't quite fit the melody floating from your guitar (or piano or bagpipe or whatever). Well, the answer is simple. Don't force it. And besides, you now have a bonus. You have the makings of two songs. Write new words for the melody you started with and then go back later and write a new melody to fit your original lyrics. And just because you've learned some new chords doesn't mean you have to use them in your next six songs. I remember the first time I experimented with Open C tuning. I found myself trying to write all of my new songs using this "new found toy". But I guarantee it doesn't work that way. Chrome wheel spinners don't necessarily look great on a rusty old Ford pickup.

**SOMETHING TO WRITE A SONG ABOUT:**
Picking the peanuts out of a cracker jack box.

**A WORD OR TWO TO INSPIRE YOUR NEXT SONG:**
Bride (Bold Bachelors Blush at Blissful Brides)

**GREAT LINES FROM GREAT SONGS:**
"Do you believe in rock and roll, can music save your mortal soul?"
– Don McLean (*American Pie*)

## SONG TITLES:

391. **I Know I'm Not the Only One**
392. **I Know Things That You Don't Know**
393. **I Miss You the Most When You're Still Here**
394. **I Never Caught a Falling Star**
395. **I Remember Mary**
396. **I Saw Santa At The Bar Drinkin' Whiskey**
397. **I Say I Love You But You Won't Let Me**
398. **I Should Have Danced With You Instead of Your Mother**
399. **I Talk to You But You Don't Hear**
400. **I Think It's Gonna Snow**

## SONGWRITING TIP #40:

Having trouble writing your current song because you can't seem to find the right rhyme? And you really love the line you have and can't seem to let go of it? Then stop trying to rhyme! Write your lyrics and let the words come as you try to express your thoughts. Once your have several lines in verse form you can go back and rearrange and re-write lyrics so they'll rhyme, but at least now you have yourself the basis for a song. Go ahead and work on the rest of the song. If the rhymes only come for certain lines, don't let it bother you. Just get the song finished in as complete a form as you can. This is also the time to strengthen your weak lines and weak rhymes. (And remember, there a some songs that don't rhyme at all.) Write and re-write. It's the only way to get the best possible song you can.

## SOMETHING TO WRITE A SONG ABOUT:

You're in Nashville, but your guitar is in Texas.

## A WORD OR TWO TO INSPIRE YOUR NEXT SONG:

Angry (Angry Activists Acting Abnormally)

## GREAT LINES FROM GREAT SONGS:

"I've never seen a night so long when time goes crawling by, the moon just went behind a cloud to hide its face and cry."
– Hank Williams (*I'm So Lonesome I Could Cry*)

## SONG TITLES:

401. **I Think She Said She Loves Me But I'm Not Sure**
402. **I Thought I Saw an Angel**
403. **I Want to Feel That Tingle**
404. **I Was Ambushed**
405. **I Was Waitin' At the Station for a Train**
406. **I Wish It Could Be Me**
407. **I Wonder What Become of Judy Ann?**
408. **I Would Die If I Could Spare the Time**
409. **I'd Buy Her New York City If I Could**
410. **I'd Rather Be Dead Than Dying**

## SONGWRITING TIP #41:

Another great source for inspiration is reading. Most of us don't read near as much as we used to. Maybe it's because we have too much on our plates nowadays. Maybe modern life has molded us a little too much into techno geeks. But there's still nothing like a good book to set the blood boiling or the mind racing. Pick up a novel by your favorite author or re-read one of your favorite books from the past. Not only does good fiction set the mind free to explore whatever world the author is creating, it also begins the mind wandering in its own direction, ready for some creativity of its own. Now this may seem like an extreme case of a lot of time spent in return for a song, but hey, it's time you read another good book anyway. Heck, it might even become a habit.

## SOMETHING TO WRITE A SONG ABOUT:

Watching children playing without a care in the world.

## A WORD OR TWO TO INSPIRE YOUR NEXT SONG:

Winchester (Winchesters Were Widespread in the Wild West)

## GREAT LINES FROM GREAT SONGS:

"Laughing like children, living like lovers, rolling like thunder, under the covers, and I guess that's why they call it the blues."
– Elton John/Bernie Taupin (*I Guess That's Why They Call It The Blues*)

## SONG TITLES:

411. **I'd Stake All I Got on You**
412. **If I Cry**
413. **If Wishes Were Horses Then Beggars Would Ride**
414. **If You're a Psycho, Read My Fortune**
415. **I'm A Little Bit Concerned About That Look There In Your Eyes**
416. **I'm Gonna Miss You When You're Gone**
417. **I'm Here Where You Ain't**
418. **I'm in Love with the Weather Girl**
419. **I'm Just a Carbon Copy on Twenty Pound Bond**
420. **I'm No Hero, But You Sure Are Super**

## SONGWRITING TIP #42:

Have you ever written a song with a first line like "I woke up this morning" or some similar "throw away" line? I know I have. I know it's hard to get started sometimes and we accept a weak line for the simple reason it gets the juices flowing, but at some point you should go back and strengthen that first line. Remember, the first line of your song should be an attention getter whether you're performing in front of a live audience or an agent or producer is listening to your song in Nashville. A "throw away" first line usually leads to a "throw away" song.

## SOMETHING TO WRITE A SONG ABOUT:

Visiting your grandma and grandpa on a Sunday afternoon.

## A WORD OR TWO TO INSPIRE YOUR NEXT SONG:

Surrender (Supernatural Surrender)

## GREAT LINES FROM GREAT SONGS:

"Once upon a time there was light in my life, now there's only love in the dark, nothing I can say, a total eclipse of the heart."
– Jim Steinman (*Total Eclipse Of The Heart*)

**SONG TITLES:**
421. **I'm Not Afraid of Flying**
422. **I'm Not Me Today**
423. **I'm Not So Sure This Is Even Where I Live**
424. **Imposter of Love**
425. **In A Backroom of My Mind**
426. **In Case of the Blues**
427. **In Deed I Do For You**
428. **In Shades of Black and White**
429. **In Some Other Mind**
430. **In the Darkness of Your Mind**

**SONGWRITING TIP #43:**

Here's a trick I use occasionally when I want to write a song but the melody is being evasive. I simply sit down and turn on the radio. Then I begin jumping from station to station until a melody strikes my fancy. Now I'm talking about the melody to a song I haven't heard before so it really doesn't work to listen to an oldies station. Listen to a station you usually don't listen to. When you hear a tune you like, turn off the radio and hum it to yourself for a moment or two. Then wait for an hour or so and see if you can recall the tune. You usually can't fully recall it, but you will usually end up with a new melody line to get your next song started. And once you put your own words to the creation and add guitar or piano chords, you will have a nifty new song sounding nothing like the one that inspired it in the first place.

**SOMETHING TO WRITE A SONG ABOUT:**

Getting caught in a rainstorm without any cover.

**A WORD OR TWO TO INSPIRE YOUR NEXT SONG:**

Cold (Cocaine Is Cold And Calculating)

**GREAT LINES FROM GREAT SONGS:**

"People are lonely, and only animals with fancy shoes."
– Jack Johnson (*The Horizon Has Been Defeated*)

## SONG TITLES:
431. **In The Darkness of a Lonely Evening**
432. **In The Evening by the River Without You**
433. **In the Event of Me Leaving You**
434. **In The Winter of our Years**
435. **Indeed I Do For You**
436. **Interviews**
437. **Into the Light**
438. **Inventor of the Smile**
439. **Is It Hot In Here? (Or Is the Sun Exploding?)**
440. **Is That Really Me in the Mirror?**

## SONGWRITING TIP #44:

Remember who you are writing for. I know many songwriters who say they only write to please themselves. Well, while this may be, the truth is that the chances of those songwriters ever having a hit on their hands is highly unlikely. The truth is if you want to be a successful songwriter you have to remember you are writing for thousands of other people. I entered a songwriting contest several years back and was pleased to learn I was one of the finalists. But when my song didn't win the competition I wondered why and wasn't too proud to ask one of the judges what the song lacked to make the final cut. His answer was that the song didn't have a bridge where the judges thought there should be one. Oh, I had a chorus, but there was no bridge. I didn't really agree with them, but it does go to show that the commercial song usually fits a pattern. I later added a bridge just for the heck of it but still find myself performing the song in its original form.

## SOMETHING TO WRITE A SONG ABOUT:
Having a snowball fight after school and being late for dinner.

## A WORD OR TWO TO INSPIRE YOUR NEXT SONG:
Anthem (Anthem For Angels and Alcoholics)

## GREAT LINES FROM GREAT SONGS:
"If I could read your mind, what a tale your thoughts could tell."
– Gordon Lightfoot (*If You Could Read My Mind*)

**SONG TITLES:**
441. **It Ain't Exactly Heaven (But It's Close Enough)**
442. **It Might Have Been Magic (But I Think It's the Beer)**
443. **It Must Be the Magic of a Million Other Loves**
444. **It Still Snows In December**
445. **It's A Gas**
446. **It's a Lonely Boat to Row Alone**
447. **It's A Long, Long Fall When You Fall Out Of Love**
448. **It's a NASCAR Kind of Night**
449. **It's Bittersweet**
450. **It's Cheaper Than Telling the Truth**

**SONGWRITING TIP #45:**
Make sure your lyrics are as strong as you can make them. Write and re-write. If you accept the first lines that come to mind and blindly label your song finished the chances are you are creating a weak song. And it will remain a weak song until you make it do its push-ups and pull-ups so it can get stronger and livelier. If you have a weak line in a verse throw it out. If you have an entire verse that's weak, write another and toss out the old one. Take the time to study your lyrics. Read them aloud as if they were poetry. Is the tempo nice and even? Do the words flow together and fit as they should? Do the words move you? Are they clever? Are they original? If not, it's time to get out the old wrench and do some serious adjustment.

**SOMETHING TO WRITE A SONG ABOUT:**
Mowing the lawn with sweat rolling down your face.

**A WORD OR TWO TO INSPIRE YOUR NEXT SONG:**
Beggar (Beggars Bargain for Bottles of Booze)

**GREAT LINES FROM GREAT SONGS:**
"Do I have to tell the story of a thousand rainy days since we first met? It's a big enough umbrella, but it's always me that ends up getting wet."
– Sting (*Every Little Thing She Does Is Magic*)

## SONG TITLES:
451. **It's For the Good of the Country Cried the Traitor**
452. **It's Hard to Stop a Train Once It Starts Rolling**
453. **It's Kinda Funny, Honey**
454. **It's Like Reading Old Love Letters**
455. **It's Not the Promises You Make, It's the Promises You Keep**
456. **It's Raining Like a River on a Cloudy Day in June**
457. **It's So Crazy**
458. **It's the Nature of the Curse**
459. **I've Been Wrong Before**
460. **I've Heard My Share of Sermons**

## SONGWRITING TIP #46:
Don't make the melodies of your songs overcomplicated. I know, we all search for something different each time we sit down to create. But a complicated melody can many times be the downfall of your song. The melody of your song should be something the audience can go home humming even if it's just a few bars. If someone hears your song several times and still can't remember bits and pieces of the melody, you've haven't written a solid song.

## SOMETHING TO WRITE A SONG ABOUT:
Fishing in a pond where you know there's no fish.

## A WORD OR TWO TO INSPIRE YOUR NEXT SONG:
Chant (Charming Chinese Children Chanting)

## GREAT LINES FROM GREAT SONGS:
"I walked under a bus, I got hit by a train. I keep falling in love, which is kinda the same."
– James Roche of Bachelor Girl (*Buses And Trains*)

## SONG TITLES:

461. **I've Held the Hoe and Pushed the Plow**
462. **I've Never Been to Nashville**
463. **I've Seen Love Come and I've Seen Love Go**
464. **Jack Benny Had a Penny**
465. **Jefferson Street Memories**
466. **Jelly Beans**
467. **Johnny and Mary Jo**
468. **John's Song**
469. **Jojo**
470. **Jukebox Baby**

## SONGWRITING TIP #47:

Seem to be having trouble coming up with a good melody for your latest creation? The words come so fast you can barely write them down, but no tune. So don't force it. Write the words now and don't be concerned with the melody at this point. Your choice is to either write the song as a poem and set it to music later or use a monotone melody so you can still set the rhythm. I've found the later choice to work better than simply writing poetry as the tempo you set will usually have an effect on your lyrics.

## SOMETHING TO WRITE A SONG ABOUT:

The smell after it rains.

## A WORD OR TWO TO INSPIRE YOUR NEXT SONG:

Chains (Chicks In Chains In Chilly Chambers)

## GREAT LINES FROM GREAT SONGS:

"A lot of people don't have much food on their tables, but they got a lot of forks and knives, and they gotta cut something."
– Bob Dylan (*Talking New York Blues*)

**SONG TITLES:**
471. **Jumpin' for Joy**
472. **Jungle Jim and Penny Loafer**
473. **Junkyard Children**
474. **Juno**
475. **Just a House Without Windows**
476. **Just Another Bad Day in Baltimore**
477. **Just Another Dead Man Lined Up on the Bar**
478. **Just Another Victim of Your Love**
479. **Just Can't Get You Off my Mind**
480. **Just Focus**

**SONGWRITING TIP #48:**

Many songwriters get stuck in the past. You shouldn't be writing songs today that sound like they were written twenty years ago. Sometimes I go back through my old tunes and play a few for the heck of it. Many of them do indeed sound like they were written 30 years ago and, of course, they were. But a few still sound fresh. This is the sign of a good song. Write a song today that will still sound good to listeners 20 years from now. Stay current. Listen to what's playing today on the radio regardless of category. Remember, the world probably isn't ready for another disco tune.

**SOMETHING TO WRITE A SONG ABOUT:**

Looking forward to Sunday football game.

**A WORD OR TWO TO INSPIRE YOUR NEXT SONG:**

Zoo (Zombie Zebras at the Zoo)

**GREAT LINES FROM GREAT SONGS:**

"When I look out my window, what do you think I see? And when I look in my window, so many different people to be."
– Donovan (*Season of the Witch*)

**SONG TITLES:**
481. **Just Foolin' Around**
482. **Just Kill Me Quick**
483. **Just Like Love**
484. **Just Like Norma Jean**
485. **Just One More Round (Before You Go)**
486. **Just Walkin' Down Kentucky Avenue**
487. **Kansas at Sundown**
488. **Keep It Slow and Easy**
489. **Keys**
490. **Kind of Crazy**

**SONGWRITING TIP #49:**
Share your music with other songwriters. It not only helps your songwriting talents to be around other songwriters, but provides a great sounding board as well. It's nice to hear friends and family say they like your music, but when other songwriters tell you they like some of your songs, well, it feels extra special. And the ego does require feeding now and then. And it is ultimately the feeding of your ego that drives you on to write your next tune. If you have paid gigs, great. Use them as a sounding board. Listen to what the audience has to say. Mingle with the audience during breaks. If you have no paid gigs find an open mike. If you have a local songwriter's group, join it. But however you do it, it is important you follow through and share your music with others. (Isn't this why you write?)

**SOMETHING TO WRITE A SONG ABOUT:**
Telling a lie and feeling guilty that you got away with it.

**A WORD OR TWO TO INSPIRE YOUR NEXT SONG:**
Cannibal (Cannibals Cook Complaining Cuisine)

**GREAT LINES FROM GREAT SONGS:**
"Something's lost, but something's gained, in living everyday."
– Joni Mitchell (*Both Sides Now*)

**SONG TITLES:**
491. **Kings and Queens and In Betweens**
492. **Kings and Queens In Old Blue Jeans**
493. **Kiss It and Make it Better**
494. **Kite String Blues**
495. **L.A.**
496. **Laces**
497. **Lady of the Avenue**
498. **Last Chance For Love**
499. **Last Stop Before Love**
500. **Late at Night While You Sleep**

**SONGWRITING TIP #50:**

If you're trying to write a song that will be commercially acceptable you should be concerned about the length of the song. Most of us have probably written an epic or two. I have more than one song running longer than five minutes. I have friends who have written songs that are even ten minutes long. None of us are Dylan so we usually can't get away with songs of epic proportions. Songs in the commercial market seldom run under two minutes and the ideal time seems to be two and a half to three minutes although anything up to approximately four minutes is acceptable in some markets. Anything longer should be something you reserve for live performances or your own CD rather than sent out to agents, producers or performers.

**SOMETHING TO WRITE A SONG ABOUT:**
Walking through a graveyard at midnight.

**A WORD OR TWO TO INSPIRE YOUR NEXT SONG:**
Desolation (Detour to Death and Desolation)

**GREAT LINES FROM GREAT SONGS:**
"Everyone is the portrait, and everyone is the brush, and everyone has the chance to change, but we never do it much."
– Stan Swanson (*It's Alright Now*)

## SONG TITLES:
501. **Laugh Like a Lover Leavin'**
502. **Laugh Lines**
503. **Lavender**
504. **Lay Those Sweet Lovin' Lips on Mine**
505. **Lazy City Afternoons**
506. **Leaning Statue of Puberty**
507. **Lear Jets and Corvettes**
508. **Leave It To The Dust and Let the Rain Settle It**
509. **Legend**
510. **Let Me Try You On For Sighs**

## SONGWRITING TIP #51:
Having trouble coming up with a melody for your latest creation? Consider setting your lyrics to an old song that is out of copyright. Songs published before 1923 are considered to be in the public domain and can be copied freely without infringement. You'd be surprised at how many times this will get you started and the rest of the melody will come on it's own. Of course, these tunes are also available to any other songwriter, but the odds are against anyone else using the same tune you do. And you'll probably find that once you're finished, your song doesn't sound much like the original anyway.

## SOMETHING TO WRITE A SONG ABOUT:
The first pet you ever had.

## A WORD OR TWO TO INSPIRE YOUR NEXT SONG:
Skeleton (Skeletons Skulking Skillfully)

## GREAT LINES FROM GREAT SONGS:
"May your hands always be busy, may your feet always be swift. May you have a strong foundation, when the winds of change shift."
– Bob Dylan (*Forever Young*)

## SONG TITLES:

511. **Let Your Lips Do the Talking**
512. **Let's Establish Some Love**
513. **Let's Go Downtown and Laugh at the People**
514. **Let's Go to the Moving Pictures**
515. **Let's Lasso An Angel and Sail Up To Heaven**
516. **Let's Play in My Chevrolet**
517. **Life After Wife**
518. **Life in Suburbia U.S.A.**
519. **Life Is Like a Kaleidoscope**
520. **Light in the Loafers**

## SONGWRITING TIP #52:

Need a new idea to fire up that songwriting engine? The simple fact is that most songs are written about people. Now it may be your lover (or ex-lover) or a friend or even that little, old lady down the street who gives you a funny cross-eyed look whenever you come out to pick up the morning paper in your underwear. (Or maybe she's simply winking. Who knows?) Where was I? Oh, yea. Try writing a song about something other than a person. Write a song about a rock or a sand castle or your underwear. All it takes is a change of pace to come up with your next tune.

## SOMETHING TO WRITE A SONG ABOUT:

The last good joke you heard.

## A WORD OR TWO TO INSPIRE YOUR NEXT SONG:

Bumblebee (Bumblebees Buzz Blissfully on Benevolent Breezes)

## GREAT LINES FROM GREAT SONGS:

"We learned more from a three minute record than we ever learned in school."

– Bruce Springsteen (*No Surrender*)

## SONG TITLES:
521. **Like a Cat with a Ball of String**
522. **Like a Clumsy Rodeo Clown**
523. **Like a Hound on the Highway**
524. **Like An Agatha Christie Book**
525. **Like an Eagle**
526. **Like Green Leaves on a Dying Tree**
527. **Like Worn Out Tires On a Gravel Road**
528. **Lilly From Philly**
529. **Linda the Beautiful**
530. **Lines**

## SONGWRITING TIP #53:
Many new songwriters believe they have either written (or will write in the near future) a song that's going to be a hit. I know I believed this for many years until reality struck me over the head with its trusty anvil. I even took cassettes and sheet music and ran around Los Angeles for a week a couple of decades ago. Now I realize the dream is usually nothing more than that. But the bottom line is you should never stop trying. It's like gambling in Vegas. If you don't put another quarter in that slot, you're never going to win the jackpot. So the secret is to write another song and then another and then another. If you're going to win the jackpot, you have to keep playing.

## SOMETHING TO WRITE A SONG ABOUT:
Trying to get out of a deal you made with the devil.

## A WORD OR TWO TO INSPIRE YOUR NEXT SONG:
Faith (Forty Philistine Followers Finally Found Faith in Philly)

## GREAT LINES FROM GREAT SONGS:
"Don't let the past remind us of what we are not now."
– Stephen Stills (*Suite: Judy Blue Eyes*)

**SONG TITLES:**
531. **Links and Chains**
532. **Lion With the Tigers**
533. **Little Bit of Nothin'**
534. **Live From Times Square**
535. **Livin' In A Vacuum**
536. **Lonely as a Mountain**
537. **Lonely Lovers Never Leave**
538. **Long Hair Flyin' In The Wind**
539. **Lookin' for an Adjective to Describe Our Love**
540. **Lookin' Out From the Inside**

**SONGWRITING TIP #54:**
Don't simply use rhymes at the end of your lines. Yes, there are many a hit song that do that, but remember, you're striving to create great stuff here. There are other places to use them as well. Try using rhymes in the middle of lines or rhyming the last two words in a line. It doesn't really matter where the additional rhymes are, but it adds something to the song. They don't even have to be perfect rhymes to make the song sound better. (A perfect rhyme is words like moon and June while close rhymes are words like moon and groom.) Or even using assonance is great. (You know, where the vowel sounds of words are similar. Like moon and clue.)

**SOMETHING TO WRITE A SONG ABOUT:**
Standing at the airport watching your lover leave.

**A WORD OR TWO TO INSPIRE YOUR NEXT SONG:**
Friends (Funny Friends with Freckled Faces)

**GREAT LINES FROM GREAT SONGS:**
"If you need someone to blame throw a rock in the air, you're bound to hit someone guilty."
– Bono and The Edge (*Dirty Day*)

## SONG TITLES:

541. **Looking For Love (But I Done Lost My Map)**
542. **Looks Like I Can Make It Without You**
543. **Loose Change**
544. **Lost in a Maze of Memories**
545. **Lost in a White Room**
546. **Lost in Love and Lovin' Every Minute**
547. **Lost In the Heartache Again**
548. **Love Ain't Enough**
549. **Love Ain't Pretty**
550. **Love Comes A-Sneakin'**

## SONGWRITING TIP #55:

Here's a great tip for improving those songs which you "think" are already finished. (Remember, it's rare that a song is truly finished.) Sit down with your guitar or at the piano and sing one of your songs as if you were performing in front of an audience. Make it feel as real as you can. Sing the song as if there were hundreds of people listening. Put as much feeling and intensity into it as you can. It's also great if you can record your song and listen to it later. You'll find that this "performance" showcases the strengths of your song and also points out areas of weakness. If you don't play an instrument sing the song a cappella. In fact, it sometimes helps to sing your songs without accompaniment when they are finished as it does away with the frills of the instrument and lets the true song shine through.

## SOMETHING TO WRITE A SONG ABOUT:

Lost on a country road in Kansas without a map.

## A WORD OR TWO TO INSPIRE YOUR NEXT SONG:

Carnival (Candy Carnivals With Caramel Carousels)

## GREAT LINES FROM GREAT SONGS:

"Lose your dreams and you will lose your mind. Ain't life unkind?"

– Mick Jagger/Keith Richards (*Ruby Tuesday*)

## SONG TITLES:
551. **Love Cult**
552. **Love For Rent**
553. **Love in Alaska In Winter**
554. **Love Is A Fatal Illness**
555. **Love Is in the Last Place You Look**
556. **Love Is Just An Alibi for Crying in Your Sleep**
557. **Love Laughs**
558. **Love Me Like There's No Tomorrow**
559. **Love Me Up a Storm**
560. **Lovers in Limbo**

## SONGWRITING TIP #56:
One thing you might try if your songs seem a bit stale or you've written your hundredth love song in a row is to completely change things up. Find a fairy tale or a legend or a good old fashion fable and play around with it. Try to write a song in first person (I, me) about the story and if that doesn't work experiment with third person perspective (he/she/it). There have been lots of great songs written about people and places whether they were true or simply tall tales. If nothing else it will get you out of that love song rut. Not that there's anything wrong with a good love song, but there's so much more to write about!

## SOMETHING TO WRITE A SONG ABOUT:
What it would be like being a clown in the circus.

## A WORD OR TWO TO INSPIRE YOUR NEXT SONG:
Lullaby (Little Ladies and Lads Like Lullabies)

## GREAT LINES FROM GREAT SONGS:
"You got to listen to the heavens, you got to try to understand. The greatness of their movement is just as small as it is grand."
– Bob Weir and John Barlow (*Walk In The Sunshine*)

**SONG TITLES:**

561. **Love's Disguise**
562. **Love's Just A Wild Stampede**
563. **Love's Like a Carousel (And I Think I'm Getting Dizzy)**
564. **Ma She's Gone and Left Me Standing Here**
565. **Main Street in Mayberry on a Saturday Night**
566. **Makin' an Appointment for Love**
567. **Mama Don't Cry**
568. **Mama's Got Me Sittin' in the Corner**
569. **Martinique on a Monday**
570. **Masque**

**SONGWRITING TIP #57:**

Another method you can use to get back on the road when you find yourself at a songwriting roadblock is to learn a couple of new chords. So you say you don't know how to play a G Major 6th let alone use it in a song? Get out the old chord book (or buy one if you don't have one) and use it in a new song. Find a chord progression that the new chord fits into comfortably and you're on your way. It addition to getting you past that songwriting roadblock, it might send you on a detour down a whole new highway as well. (You can also find plenty of internet sites with chord diagrams. Simply do a search for "guitar chords".)

**SOMETHING TO WRITE A SONG ABOUT:**

A character from the last good book you read.

**A WORD OR TWO TO INSPIRE YOUR NEXT SONG:**

Seashore (Sand at the Seashore, Sand in Your Shoes)

**GREAT LINES FROM GREAT SONGS:**

"You read your Emily Dickinson and I my Robert Frost, and we note our place with bookmarkers that measure what we've lost."
-- Simon and Garfunkel (The Dangling Conversation)

## SONG TITLES:

571. **Maybe She Loves Me, Maybe I Don't**
572. **Mecca in the Morning**
573. **Melancholy Wine**
574. **Memories I Never Knew**
575. **Midnight Song**
576. **Miss Pretty Lonely**
577. **Mists of the Mind**
578. **Mojo Magic**
579. **Molecular Dreams**
580. **Molly Might Miss Me**

## SONGWRITING TIP #58:

Having trouble coming up with lyrics to your new tune? Check out a book of poetry and try to find a poem that fits your song. Now there are two ways you can accomplish this. You can either set an existing poem to music and keep the song as such (giving credit where credit is due, of course) or you can come back at a later date and write your own lyrics when the muse allows. There's also lots of poetry available on the internet you could try to set to music and it's usually pretty easy to get in touch with the poem's author for this type of collaboration.

## SOMETHING TO WRITE A SONG ABOUT:

The front page headline from this morning's newspaper.

## A WORD OR TWO TO INSPIRE YOUR NEXT SONG:

Window (Washing Windows on Wednesday)

## GREAT LINES FROM GREAT SONGS:

"Wealthy the spirit that knows it's own flight, stealthy the hunter who slays his own fright."
– Dan Fogelberg (*Nexus*)

**SONG TITLES:**
581. **Money Don't Talk (It Whispers)**
582. **Monkey on a Tightrope**
583. **Monkeys and Mimes**
584. **Monkeys in the Bank**
585. **Monument**
586. **More of You to Go Around**
587. **Mostly in the Middle**
588. **Mostly Me**
589. **Motel Fantasy**
590. **Mourning Skies**

**SONGWRITING TIP #59:**

Stuck in the black hole of songwriter's block? Go hear some live music. It's amazing what it can do for you. Listening to your stereo can certainly provide inspiration, but there's nothing like a little live music to get the blood pumping. I'm always anxious to get home after hearing a singer/songwriter perform and pick up the guitar. It doesn't even matter how good the performers were. If they weren't good, I'm inspired to go home knowing I can create better songs. If they were fantastic it gives me something to work towards. Find out where the local coffee shops, pubs or clubs are in your area and who's playing, then make a note on your calendar. Make it a monthly outing you can look forward to. Listen to some live music on Friday night and write some great material on Saturday morning. It works!

**SOMETHING TO WRITE A SONG ABOUT:**

Your favorite food.

**A WORD OR TWO TO INSPIRE YOUR NEXT SONG:**

Dragon (Damn The Dragons! Defend The Damsel In Distress!)

**GREAT LINES FROM GREAT SONGS:**

"Everyone of them words rang true and glowed like burning coal, pouring off every page like it was written in my soul from me to you."

– Bob Dylan (*Tangled Up In Blue*)

## SONG TITLES:

591. **Movement Between Life and Death**
592. **My Fair Weather Friend On The Shore**
593. **My Love Is Deeper Than the Deepest Lake**
594. **My My My (I Saw That Look In Your Eye)**
595. **My Piece of the Sky**
596. **My Wookie Got Hooked On Heroin**
597. **Nada**
598. **Naked Like Neon**
599. **Nashville City Breakdown**
600. **Nearly Dead, But Loving Life Just the Same**

## SONGWRITING TIP #60:

So now comes the big question. Which comes first? A catchy melody so you can add words later or a great piece of prose you can eventually set to music? Simply put, the music or the words? The answer is that it doesn't really matter. Some writers write the melody first and some the lyrics. Others write both at the same time and still others bounce back and forth between them. Do whatever works for you. But most of us lean in one direction or the other. I would have to say that I write most of my melodies and lyrics at the same time although the spark is seldom quite the same. Sometimes a great title or first line will bring a melody and at other times humming a few bars in my head will bring a few words to mind. It doesn't matter, but if you find yourself creating one way or the other most of the time, try experimenting and change things up a bit. And don't forget, you could always collaborate with another writer or musician. (It sure worked well for Elton John and Bernie Taupin.)

## SOMETHING TO WRITE A SONG ABOUT:

Getting ready to jump out of an airplane for the first time.

## A WORD OR TWO TO INSPIRE YOUR NEXT SONG:

Vortex (Victim of a Violent Vortex)

## GREAT LINES FROM GREAT SONGS:

"Freedom, well, that's just some people talking. Your prison is walking through this world all alone."
– Glenn Frey and Don Henley (*Desperado*)

## SONG TITLES:
601. **Neon Tears**
602. **Never Quite Enough of Your Sweet Love**
603. **New Roads**
604. **New York Wax Museum Blues**
605. **Next to Nothing**
606. **Next Left, First Right**
607. **Nickels and Dimes**
608. **Night That Bert Killed Ernie, The**
609. **Nine O'Clock News and Ten O'Clock Blues**
610. **No Hugs For You**

## SONGWRITING TIP #61:
If there is such a thing as a hook for song lyrics, then there surely must be a musical counterpart, right? Well, sort of. But it doesn't have anything to do with the melody that accompanies your lyrics. It's called a riff and most guitarists know exactly what it is. (A simple definition of a "riff" is a short melodic phrase that may be repeated and played as a solo or used as an accompaniment.) I mean, who doesn't remember the pounding guitar part accompanying the Rolling Stones' "Satisfaction" or the great riff in Cream's "Sunshine Of Your Love"? So next time you're sort of stuck in a songwriting rut, write a guitar (or piano) riff and create a song around it. A good riff, like a good hook, will seldom be forgotten.

## SOMETHING TO WRITE A SONG ABOUT:
The first time you fell out of love.

## A WORD OR TWO TO INSPIRE YOUR NEXT SONG:
Ballerinas (Ballerinas In Beautiful Ballrooms)

## GREAT LINES FROM GREAT SONGS:
"There's no success like failure, and failure's no success at all."
– Bob Dylan (*Love Minus Zero*)

## SONG TITLES:

611. **No Sugar In My Coffin Please**
612. **Nobody Has a Clue (There's Only Me and You)**
613. **Nobody Needs Me But You**
614. **Not Much Chance of Changin'**
615. **Nothin' Cuter Than Puppies**
616. **Nothing Can Change the Future**
617. **Nothing's Fair When It Comes to Love**
618. **Nuff Said**
619. **Nylon Dreams**
620. **Oh Kay**

## SONGWRITING TIP #62:

Have you ever entered a songwriting contest? I'm not a big proponent of them in general and you should examine each one carefully because some of them are less than valid contests. Oh, there might be a prize of some sort offered, but many of these contests make their money from entry fees and could care less about who wins. But I'd still recommend entering one or two occasionally if the entry fee is reasonable. Now for the twist. I'm not suggesting you enter these contests with the idea of winning. I'm suggesting you do it because it hones your songwriting skills. You will find you put more effort into that new song if you think people are going to hear and judge it. Use it as a tool, not a means to an end and I think you'll see what I'm talking about. Hey, if you get a good song out of the deal, it was money well spent. If you happen to win a contest or two, so much the better.

## SOMETHING TO WRITE A SONG ABOUT:

What it might feel like to be an sparrow.

## A WORD OR TWO TO INSPIRE YOUR NEXT SONG:

Fog (Fingers of a Frosty Fog)

## GREAT LINES FROM GREAT SONGS:

"A dream is like a river ever changing as it flows, and a dreamer's just a vessel that must follow where it goes.
– Garth Brooks and Victoria Shaw (*The River*)

## SONG TITLES:

621. **Old Fashion Love**
622. **On Remote**
623. **On the Boulevard**
624. **One More Minute Please (Then You Can Stomp My Heart)**
625. **Open Another Can of Worms**
626. **Open Up Your Wings and Take the Leap**
627. **Orion's Last Dream Was of You**
628. **Over Easy**
629. **Over on the Other Side**
630. **Over the Line**

## SONGWRITING TIP #63:

I love assonance and alliteration. You can probably tell by many of the titles and samples I've included in this book. Songs beg for you to use them. Assonance is simply the use of similar vowel sounds repeated in successive or proximate words containing different consonants. For example: "Fleet feet sweep by sleeping sheep." Alliteration, on the other hand, is words beginning with the same sound. For example: "Many men make mountains out of molehills". Try and use them both when writing your next song. Pam Tillis had a huge hit with a song called *"Maybe It Was Memphis"*. Do you think it would have been the same great song with a title like *"Maybe It Was Chattanooga"* or how about a song titled "The Memphis Choo Choo" for that matter?

## SOMETHING TO WRITE A SONG ABOUT:

What it might feel like to be a kid again.

## A WORD OR TWO TO INSPIRE YOUR NEXT SONG:

Sandstorm (Sandstorm in my Sneakers)

## GREAT LINES FROM GREAT SONGS:

"It's a little like a lunatic lookin' like he's got some time to kill."

– Stan Swanson (*Some Things Never Change*)

**SONG TITLES:**
631. **Overture in Love Minor**
632. **Painting Night On My Windows**
633. **Palindrome**
634. **Paper or Plastic**
635. **Paper Sails**
636. **Park Bench Blues**
637. **Pay Me Back With Kindness (And Maybe a Kiss or Two)**
638. **Penny Prophet**
639. **Percolator Blues**
640. **Perfect Love**

**SONGWRITING TIP #64:**

Let the rhythm rock you! If you're writing a song and the melody doesn't seem to be working or the lyrics seem to drag, try changing the tempo of your song. Use a pounding rhythm instead of a gentle one. You say the new rhythm doesn't fit the words? So change them and save the original lyrics for another time. You might even experiment with changing the time of your song. If you're writing a song in 4/4 time, try 3/4 time and see what happens. If you bring a more up tempo beat to your tune, it will usually drive the song home. Besides, you don't want to write love songs and lullabies the rest of your life, do you?

**SOMETHING TO WRITE A SONG ABOUT:**

What it must have been like to have been Leonardo da Vinci.

**A WORD OR TWO TO INSPIRE YOUR NEXT SONG:**

Leviathan (Lumbering Leviathans Like Large Labyrinths at Lower Latitudes)

**GREAT LINES FROM GREAT SONGS:**

"My wife ran off with my best friend, and I sure do miss him."
– Phil Earhart (*My Wife Ran Off With My Best Friend*)

**SONG TITLES:**
  641. **Pipe Dreams**
  642. **Please Stay a Little Longer**
  643. **Please Don't Cry**
  644. **Please Hear My Confession**
  645. **Plenty of Time for Nothing**
  646. **Poor Peter's Blues**
  647. **Popcorn and Candy**
  648. **Prayer in 2/4 Time**
  649. **Presto! Changeo!**
  650. **Pretty Girl**

**SONGWRITING TIP #65:**
  Does your song have a payoff? Or is it like a hundred other songs? It's nice, but maybe a bit predicable. Songwriting can be compared to playing the lottery. You're usually lucky if a single number matches. But when you match three, four or five... well, your heart starts pounding a little harder, doesn't it? Make your next song a winner. Lead up to an ending or a final line that isn't expected. I'm not saying you should do this each time you write a song and in many instances it really doesn't work, but when it all comes together it's like money in the bank.

**SOMETHING TO WRITE A SONG ABOUT:**
  You're an alien from Mars meeting a human for the first time.

**A WORD OR TWO TO INSPIRE YOUR NEXT SONG:**
  Shelter (Seeking Shelter in Sheboygan)

**GREAT LINES FROM GREAT SONGS:**
  "Standing on the moon with nothing left to do. Lovely view of heaven, but I'd rather be with you."
  – Jerry Garcia and Robert Hunter (*Standing On The Moon*)

**SONG TITLES:**
651. **Pretty Girls Never Cry**
652. **Promises You Made, Promises You Broke**
653. **Puff**
654. **Pullin' All the Right Strings**
655. **Pure Love**
656. **Questions I Wish I Had Asked**
657. **Questions Without Answers**
658. **Quick! Kiss Me One More Time!**
659. **Quickly As I Quietly Go**
660. **Quietly Cryin' My Heart Out**

**SONGWRITING TIP #66:**
Are clichés good or bad? My opinion is that it's better to avoid using them completely. And yes, there are thousands of hit songs that have used clichés and there will certainly be thousands more. But why settle for the obvious when you can create something unique? Maybe you might create something so good that someday it becomes a cliché. It's not impossible. You simply have to work at it. Here's a good exercise. Think of a cliché and then change it to create something different. It doesn't even matter if it ends up meaning the same thing. Take a line like "Life Is Like a Box of Chocolates". It could become "Life Is Like a Bowl of Beans" or "Life Is Like a Shoe With a Rock In It."

**SOMETHING TO WRITE A SONG ABOUT:**
Playing seven card draw and drawing to an inside straight.

**A WORD OR TWO TO INSPIRE YOUR NEXT SONG:**
Rattlesnake (The Rattlesnake Razzledazzle)

**GREAT LINES FROM GREAT SONGS:**
"I wish I was an English muffin, 'bout to make the most out of a toaster."
– Paul Simon (*Punky's Dilemma*)

## SONG TITLES:

661. **Raincoat Robber**
662. **Raise Your Hand If You Love Me**
663. **Ramble Gamble Die**
664. **Random Thoughts**
665. **Ratchet**
666. **Ready for Rainbows, But Only Getting Wet**
667. **Really, Really Wrong**
668. **Reruns of a Kiss**
669. **Rest A Final Rest Until the Lovely**
670. **Ribbons in Your Hair**

## SONGWRITING TIP #67:

If you're looking for a subject to write a song about, try writing a tune about your mother or your father. This may or may not be a flattering tune (depending on your childhood), but the idea should inspire something on some level. It could be a generic song (good, bad or indifferent) or it could be a specific incident that happened when you were growing up. It might simply be remembering the smells in your mom's kitchen or the day your dad taught you to ride a bicycle. Or how about the time he put you in a barrel and rolled you over Niagara Falls. Good times, my friend, good times... There are probably dozens of songs ready and waiting on this subject, so warm up your fingers.

## SOMETHING TO WRITE A SONG ABOUT:

You are bored out of your mind watching daytime television.

## A WORD OR TWO TO INSPIRE YOUR NEXT SONG:

Treasures (Treasures in Trashy Trousers)

## GREAT LINES FROM GREAT SONGS:

"Clowns to the left of me, jokers to the right, here I am stuck in the middle with you."
– Joe Egan/Gerry Rafferty (*Stuck In The Middle With You*)

## SONG TITLES:

671. **Rich Girl**
672. **Ricochet**
673. **Ride the Lightning**
674. **Rings of Silver, Hair of Gold**
675. **Rip Out My Heart (And Call It A Quickie)**
676. **Robot Love**
677. **Rolling Into Tulsa**
678. **Rolling Like a Tumbleweed**
679. **Routine Is The Primary Assassin of Passion**
680. **Run With the Bang of the Gun**

## SONGWRITING TIP #68:

A tool songwriters probably don't use enough is a tape recorder. (Or a digital recorder if you can afford to take that next step.) In addition to it being a great tool for recording your song in the early stages (so you don't forget the melody or that cool guitar riff), it's also great for hearing the parts of your song that might seem weak and require re-working. What words sound awkward? What phrases don't fit? What melody is too dry or too complicated? Listen as if you hadn't written the song and, most importantly, be objective! When your song is complete make a clean tape of it. Keep your tapes organized so you know where different versions are. Do the same with songs that are incomplete. If you have a couple of great lines, but nothing else at that particular time, record and index it so you can find it later. Also keep lines, chords and tablature notations written down. You can even cross-index them to your tapes. If you have a PC there are some great recording tools you can use making it easy to stay organized. (Check them out in our resource section.)

## SOMETHING TO WRITE A SONG ABOUT:

You're a super hero that has suddenly lost his super powers.

## A WORD OR TWO TO INSPIRE YOUR NEXT SONG:

Jackpot (Just Jesus and Jackpots)

## GREAT LINES FROM GREAT SONGS:

"I asked him for mercy, he gave me a gun."
– Mickey Hart, Robert Hunter and Bob Weir (*Greatest Story Ever Told*)

## SONG TITLES:

681. **Runnin' for Shelter**
682. **Runnin' in the Red Zone**
683. **Running Down Deserted Beaches**
684. **Rust of a Thousand Tears**
685. **Sad Eyes**
686. **Sadly**
687. **Sally Sang a Sad Song**
688. **Standing by the Streetlight Looking Lonely**
689. **Saturday My Dreams All Died**
690. **Savior**

## SONGWRITING TIP #69:

Do you write songs for yourself or do you write them with the hope that one day someone else might perform or even record them? If you write for yourself then this tip isn't really relevant, but if you write songs hoping others will perform them at some point then you should keep the following in mind. Don't write about something that means something only to you and hope that other singers will understand the emotions attached. You should also keep your songs to an octave and a half at most. This is the average range for most singers.

## SOMETHING TO WRITE A SONG ABOUT:

You're John Wilkes Booth waiting in the rear of Ford Theater.

## A WORD OR TWO TO INSPIRE YOUR NEXT SONG:

Mustang (Midgets with Michelob in Mustangs Don't Mix)

## GREAT LINES FROM GREAT SONGS:

"I see my light come shining from the west unto the east. Any day now, any day now, I shall be released."
– Bob Dylan (*I Shall Be Released*)

## SONG TITLES:
691. **Say Hello to Your Mother For Me**
692. **Scaffold Blues**
693. **Searching For Happiness (Finding Sorrow)**
694. **Seas I've Sailed and Rivers I've Rowed**
695. **Secretly Saying Grace in a Greasy Spoon**
696. **Sex Is A Lot Like Singing A Song**
697. **Shades of Sorrow**
698. **Shadows of a Former Love**
699. **Shake, Shook and Shaken**
700. **Shallow Water**

## SONGWRITING TIP #70:
Can't seem to get started on a new song? You're ready to go and your fingers are itching, but nothing seems to be popping into your head other than images of a huge Philly cheesesteak with a side of home-style fries. (Now, there's a song waiting to be written.) Well, here's the solution. First, go eat lunch. Then find a book with some great pictures in it and start flipping through it. Travel books and magazines are great. Or find yourself a book with a collection of masterpieces by great artists? Check out a Picasso or Gauguin and see if maybe the muse doesn't pop up her inquisitive little noggin.

## SOMETHING TO WRITE A SONG ABOUT:
A time when you were physically sick or injured.

## A WORD OR TWO TO INSPIRE YOUR NEXT SONG:
Cardsharp (Canny Cardsharps Counting Coins)

## GREAT LINES FROM GREAT SONGS:
"Goldfish have no memory, I guess their lives are much like mine. And the little plastic castle is a surprise every time."
– Ani Difranco (*Little Plastic Castle*)

**SONG TITLES:**
701. **Sharin' the Load**
702. **Sharpshooter**
703. **Shattered Mind**
704. **She Can't Sit Still**
705. **She Could Be The One**
706. **She Couldn't Even Afford A Stamp For a Dear John Letter**
707. **She Dreams**
708. **She Is Warm in My Arms as She Sleeps**
709. **She Knows How to Giggle, She Knows How to Grin**
710. **She Knows You're A Dreamer**

**SONGWRITING TIP #71:**
This one is important. Have fun with your music. Have fun when you write your songs. Don't be afraid to write a funny or humorous song. Life doesn't always have to be serious. This is especially true of some songwriters. I've met songwriters who can quip and joke with the best of them, but when they start writing they become much too serious. Now all of your songs can't be cute and funny. We're not trying to be Ray Stevens or Weird Al Yankovic, but if you haven't tried to write a humorous song, give it a go. It can be lots of fun. And if you're a performing songwriter, you will find audiences love these numbers. Hey, if you can make an audience grin and laugh, you've won them over for the evening.

**SOMETHING TO WRITE A SONG ABOUT:**
You're granted three wishes and you only have one left.

**A WORD OR TWO TO INSPIRE YOUR NEXT SONG:**
Harlot (Heroes in Hell and Harlots in Heaven)

**GREAT LINES FROM GREAT SONGS:**
"I set my monkey on the log, and ordered him to do the Dog. He wagged his tail and shook his head, and he went and did the Cat instead."
– Bob Dylan (I Shall Be Free #10)

## SONG TITLES:
711. **She Laughed Because I Cried**
712. **She Likes a Full Moon (I Like a Dark Night)**
713. **She Moves Like Gravy in the Bowl**
714. **She Owns Me**
715. **She Say No, I Say Yes (The Best I Can Do Is Maybe I Guess)**
716. **She Shines**
717. **She Thinks She Walks On Water**
718. **Sheets**
719. **She's a Blast**
720. **She's a Classic**

## SONGWRITING TIP #72:
Avoid words that date your song. Groovy was a common word back in the sixties and early seventies, but songs that use that term now definitely date themselves. A song written before World War I with the phrase "23 skidoo" in it doesn't make sense to most people today. (If you're curious, the phrase means to leave quickly or to get out while the getting's good.) It is this problem that could date a lot of the current rap and hip hop music. Many of the words and phrases used in those songs will most likely be outdated in another decade or two.

## SOMETHING TO WRITE A SONG ABOUT:
There's blood on your hands, but you're not bleeding.

## A WORD OR TWO TO INSPIRE YOUR NEXT SONG:
Stranded (Strangers Stranded on Streetcars)

## GREAT LINES FROM GREAT SONGS:
"Across my dreams, with nets of wonder, I chase the bright elusive butterfly of love."
– Bob Lind (*Elusive Butterfly*)

## SONG TITLES:
721. **She's a Knockout**
722. **She's A Movin' Thing**
723. **She's a Real Spellbinder**
724. **She's A Work of Art**
725. **She's An Itty Bitty Bundle of Love**
726. **She's Better Than a Prize in a Crackerjack Box**
727. **She's Easy**
728. **She's Got Her Reasons, I Got Mine**
729. **She's Got Picasso In Her Living Room**
730. **She's Like Lightning**

## SONGWRITING TIP #73:

Have you ever written a song that made someone cry? (And I don't mean simply because the song was that bad!) That's your challenge. Write a song with strong emotion. Maybe it's a song about someone who has passed away that you loved dearly. Maybe it's a song that speaks of how the love of your life moved on without you. Maybe it's a song about your first born. Whatever that topic might be has the power to bring emotion (a close friend of inspiration) to the surface. Try it. Make the words strong to match the feelings you remember. It's a challenge, but if it works, you'll have a song that will touch the heartstrings of anyone who hears it.

## SOMETHING TO WRITE A SONG ABOUT:
Skipping stones across a lake.

## A WORD OR TWO TO INSPIRE YOUR NEXT SONG:
Aspen (Aspens Ain't Art in April or August)

## GREAT LINES FROM GREAT SONGS:
"Even telepathic children have to eat their vegetables."
-- Paul Kantner of Jefferson Starship (*Wild Eyes*)

**SONG TITLES:**
731. **She's Like Money in the Bank**
732. **She's Out on the Town**
733. **She's the Pick of the Litter**
734. **Ships In A Bottle**
735. **Should Have Been Me**
736. **Shuffleboard Blues**
737. **Shut Up and Say You Love Me**
738. **Signs of Love and Hate**
739. **Silver Bird**
740. **Simple as Sin**

**SONGWRITING TIP #74:**

If you don't own a drum machine (or perhaps a keyboard with a built-in drum machine) you should invest in one. There are some fairly inexpensive models available and they can do wonders for your songwriting. Experiment with different tempos. Select a rhythm at random and begin playing along. And if you own a PC and have internet access there are several virtual drum machines that you can either download or use while online. Some of these have a cost attached but some are free. Experimenting with different rhythms, tempos and sounds on a drum machine while you are songwriting will get you a more diverse song than writing without one.

**SOMETHING TO WRITE A SONG ABOUT:**
There's a door in your attic you never noticed before.

**A WORD OR TWO TO INSPIRE YOUR NEXT SONG:**
Canyon (Clumsy Climbers Cling Close to Canyon Cliffs)

**GREAT LINES FROM GREAT SONGS:**
"Each of us has his own special gift and you know this was meant to be true. And if you don't under estimate me, I won't under estimate you."
-- Bob Dylan (*Dear Landlord*)

## SONG TITLES:

741. **Siren**
742. **Sittin' in the Closet**
743. **Sittin' in the Middle of the Road Goin' Nowhere**
744. **Sittin' on a Log Countin' Lizards**
745. **Skeleton Dance**
746. **Skinny Skank**
747. **Skipping Stones**
748. **Sleep Without Dreams is Like Me Without You**
749. **Sleepytime Girl**
750. **Slide**

## SONGWRITING TIP #75:

Inspiration comes in many forms. Many times it pops up when we least expect it. A few words peek out from the recesses of our mind and suddenly a song forms. A melody drifts through a few layers of grey matter and the song takes flight. It is up to you to recognize inspiration and invite in it before it sneaks away again. It might come in the form of a comment made by a stranger in a passing crowd. It might come from something a small child says out of innocence. It might come in a moment of passion. It is your job to recognize and remember the moment so you can write about it later.

## SOMETHING TO WRITE A SONG ABOUT:

You don't recognize someone, but they seem to know you.

## A WORD OR TWO TO INSPIRE YOUR NEXT SONG:

Secret (The Secret to Successful Songwriting)

## GREAT LINES FROM GREAT SONGS:

"Dark cloud gathering, breaking the day, no point running cause it's coming your way."
-- Deep Purple (*Stormbringer*)

**SONG TITLES:**
751. **Slidin' Down a Rainbow**
752. **Smashed Like an Atom**
753. **Smiles In My Pocket**
754. **Smooth As Smooch**
755. **Snakes Can't Walk, But Snakes Can Dance**
756. **So Inviting, So Exciting**
757. **So Many Crosses to Bear**
758. **So Sweet**
759. **Socks Without Mates Are Lonely For Life**
760. **Soda Cap Medals**

**SONGWRITING TIP #76:**

The chorus of your song should not be long and wordy. Save the verbiage for the verses. That's where you're really telling the story. The chorus is where you bring things together and sum everything up. The fewer the words in your chorus and the shorter the lines, the easier it will be to remember. A good chorus could have as few as two lines in some cases, although 4 to 6 seems to be an average. It should seldom have as many as eight lines unless the lines themselves are short in construction. The fewer the words and the clearer the meaning, the better your chorus. And 99 times out of a hundred, your song title should either be the hook or should appear in the chorus. It's how listeners remember songs. A song called "A Melody in D Minor" will seldom be remembered if the line doesn't appear in the song. It also usually means that your song actually doesn't contain a line good enough to be your title or hook. How can someone buy your record or request your song if they can't remember its name?

**SOMETHING TO WRITE A SONG ABOUT:**
Riding on a Harley with the wind blowing in your face.

**A WORD OR TWO TO INSPIRE YOUR NEXT SONG:**
Waterfall (Waterfall Wishes)

**GREAT LINES FROM GREAT SONGS:**
"Mars ain't the kind of place to raise your kids, in fact it's cold as hell."
-- Elton John and Bernie Taupin (*Rocket Man*)

**SONG TITLES:**
761. **Soldier**
762. **Solid Gold**
763. **Somebody Shake Me**
764. **Somebody's At My Door Again**
765. **Somebody's Walkin' On My Grave**
766. **Someone's Cryin' In My Beer**
767. **Something About A Highway**
768. **Somewhere East of Nowhere**
769. **Somewhere In A Magazine**
770. **Somewhere It's Raining**

**SONGWRITING TIP #77:**

I mentioned earlier that learning a little music theory would be a good thing, but you shouldn't get lost in it. If you do you'll end up trying to stay within certain boundaries that should occasionally be broken. It's the bending and breaking of the rules that sometimes result in that magic spark. If you use a certain chord progression for each verse of your song, maybe you could change that chord progression in the last verse. It can add something that the audience isn't expecting.

**SOMETHING TO WRITE A SONG ABOUT:**

Describe a rainbow to a blind man.

**A WORD OR TWO TO INSPIRE YOUR NEXT SONG:**

Reflections (Refreshing Reflections of Rainbows)

**GREAT LINES FROM GREAT SONGS:**

"I believe in you, even though I be outnumbered."
-- Bob Dylan (*I Believe In You*)

**SONG TITLES:**
771. **Somewhere Someone's Laughing**
772. **Somewhere West of Wherever I Am**
773. **Song of the Crippled Angel**
774. **Songbirds**
775. **Songs and Proverbs**
776. **Songs I Could Sing If I Could Carry a Tune**
777. **Songs I Never Sing**
778. **Sort of Like Love**
779. **Sour Milk**
780. **Spank Me**

**SONGWRITING TIP #77:**

An exercise you can use when songwriting is to ask questions. This is especially useful when you find yourself spinning all four wheels and going no place fast. So let's say this is what you've got: You're watching a bus pull out of town and think you recognize a girl in the window. Now what? Ask yourself some questions about the scenario. Who is the girl? Do you know her or does she simply remind you of someone? Were you supposed to be on the bus? You could do this indefinitely and at some point the answer to one of those questions will be the next brick in the building of your song.

**SOMETHING TO WRITE A SONG ABOUT:**

Having your fortune told, but not liking what you hear.

**A WORD OR TWO TO INSPIRE YOUR NEXT SONG:**

Magic (Maybe Magic, Maybe Me)

**GREAT LINES FROM GREAT SONGS:**

"What if God was one of us, just a slob like one of us?"
-- Eric Bazilian (*One Of Us*)

**SONG TITLES:**
781. **Spend Your Life on a 747**
782. **Spinning and Weaving Your Web**
783. **Spinning Like a Top**
784. **Standin' in a Field Where the Flowers Don't Bloom**
785. **Standing At The Edge of Tomorrow**
786. **Standing In The Shadows to Hide the Tears**
787. **Standing on the Edge of Forever**
788. **Starting A Ruckus**
789. **Stasis**
790. **Steering Without Wheels**

**SONGWRITING TIP #78:**
Don't get stuck writing each one of your songs with the same rhyming scheme. You may not even realize you are doing it. If all of the cars on your block are red 4-door sedans, none of them are going to stand out from the pack. Take a look at your recent creations. Do all of your verses rhyme on the second and fourth lines? It's an easy habit to get into. You need to make some of your songs red coupes, yellow sports cars and even an occasional VW bug. Here is the short list of rhyming schemes although there are many variations. 1) Rhyming all four lines. 2) Rhyming the second and fourth lines. 3) Rhyming the first with the second and the third with the fourth. 4) Rhyming the first with the third and the second with the fourth.

**SOMETHING TO WRITE A SONG ABOUT:**
Trying to remember a fading dream.

**A WORD OR TWO TO INSPIRE YOUR NEXT SONG:**
Warrior (Will Wicked Warriors Win the War?)

**GREAT LINES FROM GREAT SONGS:**
"Star Trekin' across the universe, boldly going forward, cause we can't find reverse."
-- Graham Lister and John O'Connor (Star Trekin')

## SONG TITLES:
791. **Stick to Your Guns (But Watch Out for the Bullets)**
792. **Stick to Me Like Glue**
793. **Still Standing Where You Left Me**
794. **Still Strangers**
795. **Stone Wall**
796. **Stories**
797. **Storyteller**
798. **Stranded in the Desert Without a Coca Cola**
799. **Strange As It Seems**
800. **Stranger Things Have Happened**

## SONGWRITING TIP #80:

I use one particular method when I re-write songs that almost always improves my writing. Once I have a song and consider it pretty much finished, I go back and write additional verses. Sometimes I end up with three times as many verses as I actually need. Now I'm not really a masochist, but this really works. Then I go back and pick and choose the absolute best. Sometimes I end up combining the lines of two different verses into one improved verse. If you have some leftover lines that are still pretty good material, save them for another song. You should do this fairly early in the writing process as the more comfortable you get with a song, the harder it is to change things.

## SOMETHING TO WRITE A SONG ABOUT:
Eating a piece of freshly baked apple pie,

## A WORD OR TWO TO INSPIRE YOUR NEXT SONG:
Rabbit (Robotic Rabbits Rarely Run)

## GREAT LINES FROM GREAT SONGS:
"You don't bring me anything but down."
-- Sheryl Crow (*Anything But Down*)

## SONG TITLES:

801. **Strawman**
802. **Stuck in a Starbucks Without Any Change**
803. **Studebaker Blues**
804. **Such a Sad Place to Be**
805. **Suddenly Like Love**
806. **Suicidal Ambitions**
807. **Summer Here Summer There**
808. **Sunday Morning Music**
809. **Sunday, Monday, Tuesday**
810. **Sure of Me, Sure of You**

## SONGWRITING TIP #81:

We've discussed taking music lessons to improve your song-writing, but how about giving lessons to someone else? If you're a decent guitar player, do a little advertising and give some beginning guitar lessons. Same thing if you play keyboard. You'd be surprised at how this makes you look at things from a whole new perspective. Well, maybe the perspective isn't new, but it's definitely one you haven't viewed or thought about in awhile. Or even offer to give songwriting lessons. I don't imagine there are many music teachers offering lessons in that particular subject. And who knows, you could end up striking gold in a new talent you could collaborate with.

## SOMETHING TO WRITE A SONG ABOUT:

Watching a hummingbird.

## A WORD OR TWO TO INSPIRE YOUR NEXT SONG:

Treason (Traitors Take Treason Too Trivially)

## GREAT LINES FROM GREAT SONGS:

"There's sadness in the way the story ended, but that's the way that Billy wrote the play"
-- Stan Swanson (*Like Juliet and Romeo*)

## SONG TITLES:
811. **Sweet Thing**
812. **Systematic Failure of the Heart**
813. **Take A Left At Vegas and Head for Mexico**
814. **Take a Picture of my Mind and You Might See Me**
815. **Take Me All the Way There**
816. **Take Me to School (And Teach Me a Lesson)**
817. **Take Off Your Coat and Stay Awhile**
818. **Takin' By the Storm**
819. **Takin' it All in Stride**
820. **Taking But Not Really Stealing**

## SONGWRITING TIP #82:
Don't settle for using formulas when writing songs. Why? Because there really isn't a successful formula for writing a hit song. (If there was, someone out there would already be rich and we'd have a thousand songs sounding the same. So thank goodness there is no formula.) What I'm trying to say is to think outside the box. Take chances. Don't worry about the rules. Write a song that doesn't have a single rhyme. I actually did this some years back and it turned out to be a nice little number. No one realized the song didn't rhyme even when I mentioned the fact to the audience afterwards. In fact, there were several occasions when I had to perform the song again just to prove it. And the song wasn't as easy to write as it sounds. There were many times when the perfect rhyme popped into my head and I actually had to search for another word that didn't rhyme.

## SOMETHING TO WRITE A SONG ABOUT:
The smells in your mother's kitchen when you were a child.

## A WORD OR TWO TO INSPIRE YOUR NEXT SONG:
Rock and Roll (Rock and Roll Radio Rules)

## GREAT LINES FROM GREAT SONGS:
"You may leave here for four days in space, but when you return it's the same old place."
-- P. F. Sloan (*Eve Of Destruction*)

## SONG TITLES:
821. **Tangents**
822. **Tastes Like Chicken, Tastes Like Fish**
823. **Tattoo**
824. **Taxed to the Limit**
825. **Tears for Tomorrow**
826. **Telegram**
827. **Temptation Blues**
828. **Ten Dollar Words**
829. **Tennessee Ford Drove A Chevy**
830. **Tequila and Lime**

## SONGWRITING TIP #83:
So you haven't written a new song in over a week? A month? You say the muse has packed her suitcase and flown off to Paris to hang around the Louvre? Try this little trick. Put down the guitar or turn off the keyboard and head out to see a good movie. And by a good movie we mean one that's going to bring out some type of emotion. Going to watch "Herbie Gets Loaded" probably won't do the trick. Or is that "Herbie Fully Loaded"? Oh, well, means the same thing doesn't it? And we're not talking about going to watch killer robots invading downtown Sheboygan. We're talking about something that will invoke some feeling. Maybe it's a romantic comedy. Maybe it's a scary movie. Maybe it's a heartbreaker. If watching a movie like "The Notebook" doesn't evoke some kind of feeling then you might as well call it a night and watch an episode of the Munsters.

## SOMETHING TO WRITE A SONG ABOUT:
Sitting behind home a plate at a baseball game.

## A WORD OR TWO TO INSPIRE YOUR NEXT SONG:
Salamander (Serenade for a Salamander)

## GREAT LINES FROM GREAT SONGS:
"Down to my last dime and coming apart at the seams. I'm messed up in Mexico, living on refried dreams."
– Jim Foster and Mark Peterson (*Refried Dreams*)

**SONG TITLES:**
831. **Tequila Dreams**
832. **Texas Is No State of Mind**
833. **Thank You Mama For Packin' My Bags**
834. **That Train Doesn't Stop Here Anymore**
835. **That's the Rub**
836. **The Animal Song**
837. **The Ballad of Chris Columbus and His Dog Named Pinto**
838. **The Ballad of Obadiah Black**
839. **The Chapel of Lonely Lovers**
840. **The Clouds Get In My Eyes**

**SONGWRITING TIP #84:**

Most of us probably consider songwriting a hobby. But we also keep that faint hope alive that someday our songs will be "discovered". And if not, well, we still enjoy writing them and perhaps performing them ourselves. But songwriting is work. Maybe it doesn't seem like it at times, but it is. We seem to remember the moment we finish a song and how elated it made us feel and forget the struggles and pain that happened along the way. So you should follow the rules you would for any job. Set aside a time for your work. Eat right. Exercise regularly. And get plenty of rest. If you're banging your head against the wall at 2 a.m. in the morning because nothing's working, well, give it up. The muse is probably fast asleep in your sock drawer by now any way.

**SOMETHING TO WRITE A SONG ABOUT:**
Swimming too far from shore and you think you see a shark fin.

**A WORD OR TWO TO INSPIRE YOUR NEXT SONG:**
Anthill (Anteaters Admire Ample Anthills)

**GREAT LINES FROM GREAT SONGS:**
"Complain about the future and blame it on the past, I'd like to find your inner child and kick its little ass."
-- Glenn Frey and Don Hedley (*Get Over It*)

**SONG TITLES:**
841. **The Dancing Poet**
842. **The Days Are Dark Without You**
843. **The Devil Don't Dance, He Prances**
844. **The End of Genesis**
845. **The Execution of November**
846. **The Fantastic Flight of the Crippled Bumblebee**
847. **The First Daze of the Week**
848. **The First Time I Touched You**
849. **The Fish Ain't Biting 'Cause I Got No Bait**
850. **The Flash of the Lightning**

**SONGWRITING TIP #85:**

I've mentioned that you should learn to play an instrument if you don't already. It will aid you immensely in your songwriting. But if you already play an instrument, try this suggestion. Learn to play a different one. If you play guitar, learn to play keyboard. If you play keyboard, learn to play guitar. Most people consider these the best songwriting instruments. What if you can't afford to buy a decent guitar or keyboard? Well, then buy something cheap to experiment with. Buy a harmonica or a cheap flute or even a kazoo. I even bought one of those cheap plastic tonettes one time and got two or three numbers out of it. You'd be surprised at what a change in instruments can bring to your songwriting.

**SOMETHING TO WRITE A SONG ABOUT:**

You're trying to lose weight but that cake sure looks good.

**A WORD OR TWO TO INSPIRE YOUR NEXT SONG:**

Freedom (Fences For Freedom)

**GREAT LINES FROM GREAT SONGS:**

"Like a poem poorly written we are verses out of rhythm, couplets out of rhyme in syncopated time."
-- Paul Simon (*The Dangling Conversation*)

## SONG TITLES:
851. **The Gods Must Be Watching Over You**
852. **The Grand Mindspan of 1969**
853. **The Great Grape Escape**
854. **The Ice Lady**
855. **The Joke's On You**
856. **The Lady Loves to Laugh**
857. **The Last Time I Looked In Your Eyes**
858. **The Last Time I Saw Eden**
859. **The Last Time I Saw Her She Was Waving Goodbye**
860. **The Last Time I Say Goodbye**

## SONGWRITING TIP #86:

Don't make your lyrics overly complex. Don't use words that require a dictionary to find their meaning. Don't write your songs as if you need to prove you went to college. It's called simplicity and it works like a charm. Now simplicity doesn't mean boring. There are thousands and thousands of great words that everyone knows. Use them. Don't say "she has a corpulent posterior" when you simply want to say "she has a big butt." (I know I'm going to hear about that one!)

## SOMETHING TO WRITE A SONG ABOUT:

Watching an old man pushing his laughing wife on a swing.

## A WORD OR TWO TO INSPIRE YOUR NEXT SONG:

Ordinary (Ordinary Ogres)

## GREAT LINES FROM GREAT SONGS:

"Love on the rocks, ain't no surprise. Pour me a drink and I'll tell you some lies."
-- Neil Diamond (*Love On The Rocks*)

## SONG TITLES:

861. **The Leaves in the Trees and the Flowers in Your Hair**
862. **The Loving Lady's Gone**
863. **The Man In The Moon Is Laughin' At Me**
864. **The Mountains of my Mind**
865. **The Rock and Roll Salvation Band**
866. **The Story of Johnny Paradise**
867. **The Toad at the Side of the Road**
868. **The Truth Always Hurts**
869. **The United States of America Blues Song (The Red, White and Blues)**
870. **There Ain't No Clouds In Hell**

## SONGWRITING TIP #87:

Many songwriters neglect the importance of the song title. It is one of the most important weapons in the battle for getting your music published if that is the avenue you are trying to pursue. Publishers and performers are deluged with songs and many are never looked at or are thrown on a pile that grows higher each day in the hope that sooner or later someone will dig through it. Take care when creating your song title. If it's the same as your hook (which is usually the case) make it strong so that it stands out from the crowd. A song titled "I Love You" isn't going to get the attention it deserves even if it's one of the best in the slush pile. But a song titled "I'd Love You If I Only Knew Your Name" might at least make it to the CD or tape player.

## SOMETHING TO WRITE A SONG ABOUT:

Flying a kite with a child for the first time.

## A WORD OR TWO TO INSPIRE YOUR NEXT SONG:

Ricochet (Random Ricochets)

## GREAT LINES FROM GREAT SONGS:

"A man has one, a cat has nine, and in between it's killing time."
-- Ray Davies (*Killing Time*)

## SONG TITLES:
871. **There Ain't No Fame and There Ain't No Glory**
872. **There's a Hat on the Hat Rack (And It Ain't Mine)**
873. **There's No Certain Way to Say I Love You**
874. **There's No Tomorrow Like Today**
875. **There's Snow In the Valley**
876. **There's Some Rumors Floating 'Round**
877. **There's Something in the Air (And It Ain't Love)**
878. **They Call Him Lightning Slim**
879. **They Don't Wear Tuxedos in Texas**
880. **Three Shoes, Two Feet**

## SONGWRITING TIP #88:

Need to break out of the mold and write something a little different? We all get stuck in the middle of the pasture at times with that old bull staring us in the face and then simply stand there trying to figure out which way to run. Well, the secret is to simply start running as fast as you can. If you're a rock and roll aficionado, write a country and western song. (Hey, you don't have to brag about it to your buddies or nothing.) If you're a hip hop artist, write a slow ballad. If you're a country western songwriter, well, go get a beer and start writing. Your compadres would never let you live down the time you wrote a rock and roll song.

## SOMETHING TO WRITE A SONG ABOUT:
What it feels like to have to get up and go to work every day.

## A WORD OR TWO TO INSPIRE YOUR NEXT SONG:
Cold (Cursing In The Cold)

## GREAT LINES FROM GREAT SONGS:
"Gravedigger, when you're diggin' my grave, make it shallow so I can feel the rain."
-- Dave Matthews (*Gravedigger*)

## SONG TITLES:

881. **Through the Eyes of the Kind**
882. **Through Thick and Thin and Back Again**
883. **Thug**
884. **Thunderstorm**
885. **Tim Buck Two**
886. **Time Never Stops to Ponder the Past**
887. **Time to Cash in my Chips**
888. **Tired of Being Nobody's Baby**
889. **Too Blue For You**
890. **Too Cool**

## SONGWRITING TIP #89:

I've mentioned the songwriter's toolkit, but we haven't really talked about everything it should contain. Well, we've mentioned the essential books earlier. (Dictionary, Thesaurus, Rhyming Dictionary, etc.) You should also have the following items within reach. Paper (an 8 1/2 x 11 legal pad works great). Pens or pencils (I usually use a pen and have cross-outs and line-throughs everywhere. It makes it look like I'm actually getting something done.) Also have a tape recorder handy. Quality doesn't matter as you are simply using it to record bits and pieces or rough versions of finished songs so you don't forget them. Oh, and a musical instrument close by probably wouldn't hurt either! Chips and dip are optional. Check out our resource section at the end of the book for more information.

## SOMETHING TO WRITE A SONG ABOUT:

The first time you ever saw the ocean.

## A WORD OR TWO TO INSPIRE YOUR NEXT SONG:

Troll (The Trouble With Trolls)

## GREAT LINES FROM GREAT SONGS:

"I find it kind of funny, I find it kind of sad. The dreams in which I'm dying are the best I've ever had."
-- Roland Orzabal of Tears for Fears (*Mad World*)

## SONG TITLES:

891. **Too Drunk to Tango**
892. **Too Few Good Days, Too Many Bad Nights**
893. **Too Good to Be True**
894. **Too Late to Change Your Mind**
895. **Too Little, Too Late**
896. **Too Many Heartaches to Count**
897. **Too Much Lovin'**
898. **Too Much Money (Not Enough Love)**
899. **Too Much Temptation**
900. **Too Stupid to Care**

## SONGWRITING TIP #90:

And what do we do with prosody? And no, it doesn't concern drugs and it isn't an illness. Prosody is basically the marriage of lyric and melody. You can look at it a couple of ways. First, if you're writing a happy, go-lucky song, you probably shouldn't write it in a minor key. The same applies when writing a sad song. It should probably not be written in G Major. (And yes, there are exceptions to this rule as well.) Another explanation of prosody is to use the right note sequence with the accompanying lyrics. If you're writing a song about rising up, then your accompanying note pattern should do the same. (A good example is Jimmy Webb's "Up, Up and Away".)

## SOMETHING TO WRITE A SONG ABOUT:

Watching squirrels in the yard fighting over nuts.

## A WORD OR TWO TO INSPIRE YOUR NEXT SONG:

Hope (Hanging Onto Hope)

## GREAT LINES FROM GREAT SONGS:

"I've been searching for the daughter of the devil himself, I've been searching for an angel in white."
-- Glenn Frey/Don Hedley (*One Of These Nights*)

## SONG TITLES:

901. **Toss It Over**
902. **Toxic**
903. **Tracks**
904. **Trains I've Never Taken**
905. **Train's Off the Track**
906. **Transatlantic Homesick Blues**
907. **Trapped in the Web of Your Love**
908. **Trashcan**
909. **Trashy Girls**
910. **Travesty**

## SONGWRITING TIP #91:

How does the middle of your song feel? We've talked about making the beginning of your song strong and to strengthen the end, but don't forget about the middle. You don't want people finding this an ideal time to order another drink in the middle of your tune simply because you lost the power to hold them. (And if you're playing in a coffee house, you're going to lose to that cappuccino machine every time!) Remember, a song only contains a chorus, a few verses and maybe a bridge. If you have weak lines in the middle of your song, sharpen your pencil and get to work.

## SOMETHING TO WRITE A SONG ABOUT:

Walking through dark woods when your flashlight goes out.

## A WORD OR TWO TO INSPIRE YOUR NEXT SONG:

Paranoia (Pure Paranoia)

## GREAT LINES FROM GREAT SONGS:

"It may be the devil or it may be the Lord, but you're going to have to serve somebody."
-- Bob Dylan (*Gotta Serve Somebody*)

## SONG TITLES:
911. **Troubadour**
912. **Trouble Likes to Call Me Friend**
913. **Turning the Corner**
914. **Turnpike**
915. **Twentieth Century Song**
916. **Two A.M.**
917. **Two Strikes and Lookin' at a Fastball Again**
918. **Ugly Girls**
919. **Umbrella Love**
920. **Under Bridges, Over You**

## SONGWRITING TIP #92:

We've already mentioned listening to the radio or your favorite CD to get the juices flowing, but what happens if your last two or three (or nine or ten) songs sound too much alike? I think that happens to each of us now and again. It's like you're spinning your wheels on a gravel road and getting nowhere fast. Listening to other artists seems to help, but one trick I really like is to learn someone else's songs. Do you like Shawn Colvin? John Prine? Jack Johnson? Randy Newman? Sit down and learn one of their songs. And learn it as if you were going to play it for someone else. In other words, try to make it your own. More times than not, you will learn something that will spark your songwriting ignition whether it is a guitar part or a new chord progression.

## SOMETHING TO WRITE A SONG ABOUT:
A kid when he hears the music of an ice cream truck.

## A WORD OR TWO TO INSPIRE YOUR NEXT SONG:
Scorpion (Skittish Scorpions Scampering)

## GREAT LINES FROM GREAT SONGS:
"She leaned way back just to straighten up her hose, well the ice cream melted and the coffee froze."
-- Bob Center (*Flea Brain*)

**SONG TITLES:**
921. **Under the Thunder**
922. **Up the Creek and Down the Street**
923. **Urban Prophecies**
924. **Vacation in Virginia City**
925. **Very Nearly Naughty**
926. **Victorian Highways**
927. **Visits to Venus**
928. **Waitin' For the Sparks (Lookin' For the Fire)**
929. **Waiting for the Green Light and Running Out of Patience**
930. **Waiting 'Til the Bell Rings**

**SONGWRITING TIP #93:**

Fill your songs with good, original metaphors and paint images as if you were an artist putting brush to canvas. You are not simply picking words at random. You are painting with words. Don't settle for a two dollar word when there's a hundred dollar gem waiting for you to discover it. Use strong words that convey strong images. These are similar to the "words to inspire your next song" that I've included in this book. These are what I call "power words". They are words that startle or inspire or make you vividly see something. "She flew like a bird" isn't nearly as strong as "She sailed like an eagle". "Sailed" is a stronger verb than "flew" and "eagle" conveys a stronger image than "bird". Take a look at some of Dylan's songs and see what I mean. He uses lots of words that you wouldn't expect in a song, but he makes them work.

**SOMETHING TO WRITE A SONG ABOUT:**

Not wanting to be the first one to speak after an argument.

**A WORD OR TWO TO INSPIRE YOUR NEXT SONG:**

Rendezvous (Rendezvous With Reality)

**GREAT LINES FROM GREAT SONGS:**

"She was a long cool woman in a black dress, just a 5-9 beautiful tall. With just one look I was a bad mess, cause that long cool woman had it all."
-- Clark, Cook and Greenaway (*Long Cool Woman*)

**SONG TITLES:**
931. **Wake Me When It's Over**
932. **Walkin' Against the Wind**
933. **Walking On The River**
934. **Warm as Butter in the Sun**
935. **Watch Me Walkin' Out the Door**
936. **Watchin' a Fly on the Wall**
937. **Water Under the Bridge**
938. **Wave Your Magic Wand**
939. **Waves**
940. **We Could**

**SONGWRITING TIP #94:**

Here's something I'll bet you haven't considered. Collaborate with someone who's never written a song. Yes, you heard me right and no, I'm not crazy. (Although some say that is a matter of opinion.) It's another one of those little tools you can experiment with when the songwriting's taken a stale turn. Try writing a song with your significant other. (Hey, you never know where that might lead...) Ask a buddy if he'd be interested in trying to write a song. How about a brother or sister? If you have a creative streak, maybe they do as well. If you write great melodies, but your lyrics are mediocre, have someone write a poem and then add your melody and see what develops.

**SOMETHING TO WRITE A SONG ABOUT:**

Staring at an aquarium in a doctor's office.

**A WORD OR TWO TO INSPIRE YOUR NEXT SONG:**

Love (Lilly Likes Lulu, But Lulu Loves Leland)

**GREAT LINES FROM GREAT SONGS:**

"I had too much to dream last night."
-- Mantz/Tucker (*I Had Too Much To Dream*)

**SONG TITLES:**
941. **We Got a Sure Thing Goin' (I Think)**
942. **We Never Talk Anymore**
943. **What Could Possibly Be Better Than That?**
944. **What You Gonna Do When I'm Packed Up and Gone**
945. **When Did We Fall Out of Love?**
946. **When the Clouds Clear**
947. **When the Darkness Seeps Into Your Dreams**
948. **When the Music Moves Me**
949. **When the Odds Are Stacked Against You**
950. **When The Rock Stops Rollin'**

**SONGWRITING TIP #95:**
A great source for new song ideas is listening to other people's conversations. Now I know it isn't polite to eavesdrop, but sometimes it's impossible not to. Take advantage of these times and keep your pen and notepad handy. And remember to be discreet. That 300 pound biker at the bar might not appreciate you leaning in to hear him talking about his new pair of purple pumps.

**SOMETHING TO WRITE A SONG ABOUT:**
Being challenged by the school bully to met him after school.

**A WORD OR TWO TO INSPIRE YOUR NEXT SONG:**
Goodbye (Gotta Go, Goodbye!)

**GREAT LINES FROM GREAT SONGS:**
"All those angels running, picking up the pieces. putting back together hearts broke long ago."
-- Patty Larkin (*Good Thing*)

## SONG TITLES:
951. **When the Sun Gets in Your Brain**
952. **When The Water Rolls In**
953. **When You Hear the Sirens Singing**
954. **When You Struck Me Like a Lightning Bolt From Out of the Sky**
955. **Where You Are I Am**
956. **Whips, Chains and Cotton Candy**
957. **Whispers In The Dark**
958. **Whispers Like Wine On a Satin Sheet**
959. **White Fences in the Dark of Night**
960. **Who Burned the Bridge?**

## SONGWRITING TIP #96:
Another great way to diversify your song is to change the rhythm between your verse and the chorus or bridge. Now this doesn't mean to switch from 3/4 time to 4/4 time (as interesting as that might sound) and it definitely doesn't mean simply speeding up the song and slowing it down again. Rather it pertains more to the way you use your lyrics and the syllables of the words in the chorus and the verse. If the verse and chorus rhythms are the same, there is less to distinguish the difference between them. If your verses have long lines with lots of syllables, try using short lines with shorter syllables in your chorus. This will automatically create contrast between the different sections of your song.

## SOMETHING TO WRITE A SONG ABOUT:
The first time your parents let you stay at home alone.

## A WORD OR TWO TO INSPIRE YOUR NEXT SONG:
Sparrow (The Sorrows of Sad Sparrows)

## GREAT LINES FROM GREAT SONGS:
"You're a heartbreaker, dream maker, love taker, don't you mess around with me."
-- Geoff Gill and Clint Wade (*Heartbreaker*)

## SONG TITLES:

961. **Who Killed Barney?**
962. **Who Killed Our Love? (And Am I A Suspect?)**
963. **Who Stole My Baby?**
964. **Whoopsie Daisey**
965. **Who's Gonna Stop Us Now**
966. **Why Ain't It Friday?**
967. **Why Isn't Pie on the Menu?**
968. **Why Lover's Lane Ain't on the Map**
969. **Why Should I Trust Your Mother?**
970. **Wild and Wooly Willie**

## SONGWRITING TIP #97:

You should also try writing your songs from different points of view. Are all of your songs written in first person? ("I can't sleep with her crying like that" or "We go together like potatoes and gravy"). If you find you are constantly writing in first person, try changing things up. Write a song in second person. ("You always change your clothes, but you never change yourself".) And third person can really change a song. ("He graduated second in a class of one.") So remember: 1st person (I, me, we), 2nd person (you), and 3rd person (he, him, she, her, it, they, them).

## SOMETHING TO WRITE A SONG ABOUT:

You're trying to catch a taxi in the rain.

## A WORD OR TWO TO INSPIRE YOUR NEXT SONG:

Mansion (Mansion of Marble)

## GREAT LINES FROM GREAT SONGS:

"I see my light come shining from the west unto the east. Any day now, any day now, I shall be released."
-- Bob Dylan (*I Shall Be Released*)

## SONG TITLES:
971. **Will I Ever Laugh Again?**
972. **Windows**
973. **Wish I Was Rich**
974. **Wishin' You the Worst**
975. **Workin' on Winning Your Love**
976. **Worms**
977. **Yes I No-No**
978. **You Are Me**
979. **You Are My Destiny**
980. **You Can Hold My Interest Any Time**

## SONGWRITING TIP #98:

Many songwriters write only lyrics or music. Of course, they need someone with whom they can collaborate and that's fine and dandy. But if you fall into one of those categories why not try your hand at the rest of the bundle? If you write lyrics and don't play an instrument try learning keyboard or guitar. You can pick up used or even new keyboards and guitars fairly inexpensively. Take some lessons and see where it leads. If you write melodies but no lyrics try your hand at that. Write some poetry without trying to write song lyrics and see where it leads. If it works, great. If it doesn't, you really haven't lost anything trying.

## SOMETHING TO WRITE A SONG ABOUT:
You can't remember where you parked your car.

## A WORD OR TWO TO INSPIRE YOUR NEXT SONG:
Fingers (Feeling Phantom Fingers)

## GREAT LINES FROM GREAT SONGS:
"I was so much older then, I'm younger than that now."
-- Bob Dylan (*My Back Pages*)

## SONG TITLES:

981. **You Can Leave Any Time You Like**
982. **You Change Your Mind Like You Change Your Clothes**
983. **You Doll You**
984. **You Don't Have a Clue, Do You?**
985. **You Got Another Think Comin'**
986. **You Just Can't Cheat at the Game of Love**
987. **You Make My Water Boil**
988. **You Mean a Mustang Is Also a Car?**
989. **You Must Have Lost Your Halo Somewhere Along the Highway**
990. **You Remind Me of Mary**

## SONGWRITING TIP #99:

If you're a songwriter who plays guitar and primarily uses that instrument to create your songs, I recommend you experiment with tablature. For those that might not know what tablature is take look at a diagram for any guitar chord. That is what tablature (or tab) is in its simplest form. Tablature uses diagrams of guitar strings and frets to represent notes which translate into finger placement on the fret board. It is a way for guitarists to read music without learning traditional sheet music reading. It's sole purpose, however, is not simply for chord diagrams. It can be used to represent anything from lead guitar parts to finger picking sequences. It is handy for "jotting" down guitar parts or melodies so you don't forget them. There are many online resources for tablature as well as books on the subject. There is a learning curve, but it can be an invaluable tool.

## SOMETHING TO WRITE A SONG ABOUT:

You're in a hurry to get home, but you're caught in traffic.

## A WORD OR TWO TO INSPIRE YOUR NEXT SONG:

Bazooka (Bimbos With Bazookas)

## GREAT LINES FROM GREAT SONGS:

"Papa loved Mama, Mama loved men, Mama's in the graveyard, Papa's in the pen."
-- Garth Brooks and Kim Williams (*Papa Loved Mama*)

## SONG TITLES:
991. **You Rock Me, You Roll Me**
992. **You Send Me**
993. **Your Body's a Temple (And I Think It's Time to Pray)**
994. **Your Love Is Stronger Than Whiskey**
995. **You're a Mighty Grand View**
996. **You're Ice (I'm Fire)**
997. **You've Been Lovely Knowing Me**
998. **Zero Times Two**
999. **Zipped!**
1000. **Zombie On Ice**
1001. **Zoo Blues**

## SONGWRITING TIP #100:
Want to improve your lyrics? Set aside your music and simply read your song as if it were a poem. Does the rhythm feel right? Do your lines feel as if they have the correct number of syllables? We aren't talking about the content or meaning of your lyrics, but simply the rhythm of the syllables as they relate to each other. If you read a line and have to pause for any reason other than continuing to the next line, there is probably something wrong with your lyrics. This isn't a hard and fast rule by any means. Singing a song is different than reading poetry as you have different note combinations to work with, but I've found that it still helps to read your song aloud.

## SOMETHING TO WRITE A SONG ABOUT:
Writing a song on a guitar with a busted string.

## A WORD OR TWO TO INSPIRE YOUR NEXT SONG:
Freedom (Fanning The Flames Of Freedom)

## GREAT LINES FROM GREAT SONGS:
"If you can't be with the one you love, love the one you're with."
-- Stephen Stills (*Love The One You're With*)

## SONGWRITING TIP #101:

And so we come to our final songwriting tip. And this one's about the golden rule of songwriting. And what is the golden rule of songwriting? Well, it's simple. There are no rules. Write from the heart. Let your mind fill in the blank spots, but don't let it get in the way. If you try writing with your brain as your only tool, then you might as well be an accountant. Not that there's anything wrong with that, but if you write from the heart, you can truly call yourself a songwriter.

## SOMETHING TO WRITE A SONG ABOUT:

The feeling you get when you finish writing a good song.

## A WORD OR TWO TO INSPIRE YOUR NEXT SONG:

Tapestry (Torn and Tattered Tapestries)

## GREAT LINES FROM GREAT SONGS:

"Out past the cornfields where the woods got heavy, out in the back seat of my '60 Chevy. Workin' on mysteries without any clues, workin' on our night moves."

-- Bob Seger (*Night Moves*)

## FROM CAVEMEN TO ASTRONAUTS

There's been many an inspiration caused by either falling in or out of love. But let's face it. The muse doesn't visit happy couples near as often, does it? I mean you aren't so desperate as to pick a fight with your significant other simply to have something to write a song about, are you?

So try writing a song about somebody famous. Or even infamous. It's simple enough to do. Pick up a copy of today's newspaper or the most recent *People* magazine. You'll find plenty of news and stories that might trigger a song. Or pick up a history book and flip through the pages.

Another great source is our old friend and close family member, the television set. Keep a notebook handy and jot down interesting ideas for songs about people. You'll fill a page in no time. The Biography Channel is a great for information plus it gives you the facts you require to start writing.

One thing to keep in mind when you're writing about real people is to do your research and get your facts straight. This is especially true when writing a song about someone alive, well and willing to sue. Of course, if you write a song about Carl the Caveman you really don't have to worry about that unless they find Carl frozen in the Arctic and unfreeze him.

Many of the folks we've included in our list you probably recognize. If not, simply type the name into the Google search box (or your favorite search engine) and you'll get more than enough information to put together your next masterpiece. And remember, these "people" don't have to be real. (e.g. John Henry, Casey Jones or even John Jacob Jingleheimer Schmidt!)

You probably already believe me when I tell you that you can find some great song ideas by writing about people, but in case you have your doubts, take a look at some of these great songs.

*"Billy the Kid"* by Tom Petty
*"Galileo"* by the Indigo Girls
*"Hurricane"* by Bob Dylan.
*"Roll Over Beethoven"* by Chuck Berry
*"Bette Davis Eyes"* by Kim Carnes

## 101 People You Can Write A Song About

1. **Mark Twain**
2. **Pablo Picasso**
3. **Archimedes**
4. **Amelia Earhart**
5. **Marco Polo**
6. **Jack Benny**
7. **Atilla the Hun**
8. **Rosa Parks**
9. **Donald Trump**
10. **Frank Sinatra**
11. **Stephen Hawking**
12. **Homer Simpson**
13. **Mahatma Gandhi**
14. **P. T. Barnum**
15. **Ferdinand and Isabella**
16. **Calamity Jane**
17. **Roger Bannister**
18. **Captain Kirk**
19. **Robinson Crusoe**
20. **Dr. Jack Kevorkian**
21. **Isaac Asimov**
22. **Fred Astaire and Ginger Rogers**
23. **Walt Disney**
24. **Daffy Duck**
25. **Slim Pickens**
26. **Nicolaus Copernicus**
27. **John Wayne**
28. **Bonnie and Clyde**
29. **Jeff Gordon**
30. **Jules Verne**
31. **Henry Ford**
32. **Jackie Chan**
33. **The Lucky Charms Leprechaun**
34. **Charles Lindbergh**
35. **Robert Frost**
36. **Levi Strauss**
37. **Robert Peary and Frederick Cook**
38. **Shirley Temple**
39. **Luke Skywalker**
40. **Tinkerbell**
41. **Gomez Addams**

42. **Frank Lloyd Wright**
43. **George Burns and Gracie Allen**
44. **Pancho Villa**
45. **Mae West**
46. **Thomas Edison**
47. **Edgar Allen Poe**
48. **Abner Doubleday**
49. **Amos and Andy**
50. **Harriett Jacobs**
51. **Clark Gable and Carole Lombard**
52. **Bob Dylan**
53. **Dante Alighieri**
54. **Charlemagne**
55. **Paul Tibbets**
56. **Albert Einstein**
57. **Jackie Robinson**
58. **Captain Kangaroo**
59. **Howard Hughes**
60. **Flash Gordon**
61. **The Wright Brothers**
62. **Angelina Jolie**
63. **Ken and Barbie**
64. **Aphrodite**
65. **Muhammad Ali**
66. **Rock Hudson and Doris Day**
67. **Neil Armstrong**
68. **King Arthur**
69. **Batman and Robin**
70. **Icarus**
71. **Fred Flintstone and Barney Rubble**
72. **Clark Kent**
73. **Napoleon**
74. **Wernher Von Braun**
75. **Tiger Woods**
76. **Emily Dickinson**
77. **Jim Thorpe**
78. **St. Francis of Assisi**
79. **Johnny Appleseed**
80. **Joan of Arc**
81. **Hannibal Lector**
82. **John Gutenberg**
83. **Elvis Presley**
84. **Caligula**

85. **Popeye**
86. **Mark Twain**
87. **Louisa May Alcott**
88. **Charlie Chaplin**
89. **Dolly Parton**
90. **Zorro**
91. **Jim Morrison**
92. **Sir Walter Raleigh**
93. **Stan Laurel and Oliver Hardy**
94. **Roy Rogers and Dale Evans**
95. **Mary Fields**
96. **Martin Luther King**
97. **Betsy Ross**
98. **Lucille Ball and Desi Arnez**
99. **Pete Rose**
100. **John Smith and Pocahontas**
101. **Sebastian Bach**

## TWO TICKETS TO TIMBUKTU, PLEASE

There's no doubt that geographical locations can inspire a song. It might be anything from lounging lazily in the comfort of your own living room to lying on a beach in Australia.

Sit down with pencil and paper in hand and make a list of places you've been in your life. We aren't simply talking famous places or places you visited on your last vacation although those should certainly be on your list. How about the time you visited Uncle McDonald's farm in Kansas or took a ferry ride in the Seattle Sound? They are all valid inspirations for a song.

And nothing great even need to have happened at that particular spot. The location itself should be enough to inspire the muse. The sights. The sounds. The smells. Close your eyes and imagine you are there again.

The location doesn't necessarily have to be one you have visited or are even familiar with. Can you write about lying on the beach in Australia watching the surf roll in if you haven't been there? Well, maybe not as effectively as if you had actually visited the area, but you're a songwriter for heaven's sake. Use your imagination. Read a book about the location or visit a web site or two. Then imagine you're there and see what inspiration brings to your doorstep.

Need a few examples?

*"China Girl"* by David Bowie
*"California Dreaming"* by the Mamas and the Papas
*"Atlantis"* by Donovan
*"Walking In Memphis"* by Marc Cohn
*"Blue Bayou"* by Linda Ronstadt

### 101 Places You Can Write A Song About
1. **Abbey Road (London)**
2. **Amsterdam (Netherlands)**
3. **Antarctica**
4. **Aspen (Colorado)**
5. **Athens (Greece)**
6. **Austin (Texas)**

7. **The Bad Lands (South Dakota)**
8. **Bagdad (Iraq)**
9. **Baker Street (London)**
10. **Bali (Indonesia)**
11. **Bangkok (Thailand)**
12. **Barcelona (Spain)**
13. **Beale Street (Memphis)**
14. **Beijing (Peking) China**
15. **Berlin (Germany)**
16. **The Bermuda Triangle**
17. **Big Ben (London)**
18. **The Boardwalk in Atlantic City (New Jersey)**
19. **Bora Bora (French Polynesia)**
20. **Bourbon Street (New Orleans)**
21. **Cape Cod (Massachusetts)**
22. **Cape Town (South Africa)**
23. **Denver (Colorado)**
24. **Disneyworld (Florida)**
25. **Dublin (Ireland)**
26. **Durango (Colorado)**
27. **Eden**
28. **Edinborough (Scotland)**
29. **Eiffel Tower (Paris)**
30. **Fifth Avenue (New York)**
31. **Fisherman's Wharf (San Francisco)**
32. **The French Quarter (New Orleans)**
33. **Galapagos Islands (Ecudor)**
34. **Gettysburg Battlefield (Pennsylvania)**
35. **Graceland (Memphis)**
36. **The Grand Canyon**
37. **The Great Barrier Reef (Australia)**
38. **The Great Wall of China**
39. **Haight Street (San Francisco)**
40. **Havana (Cuba)**
41. **Heaven**
42. **Hell**
43. **Hilton Head Island (South Carolina)**
44. **Hiroshima (Japan)**

45. **Hollywood (California)**
46. **Istanbul (Turkey)**
47. **Kalahari Desert (Africa)**
48. **Kathmandu (Nepal)**
49. **Kenya (Africa)**
50. **Key West (Florida)**
51. **Kilkenny Castle (Ireland)**
52. **Kingston (Jamaica)**
53. **Krakatoa Island (Indonesia)**
54. **Lake Tahoe (California/Nevada)**
55. **Lisbon (Portugal)**
56. **Machu Picchu (Peru)**
57. **Madison Avenue (New York)**
58. **Market Street (San Francisco)**
59. **Martha's Vineyard (Massachusetts)**
60. **The Mekong Delta (Viet Nam)**
61. **Memphis (Tennessee)**
62. **Mexico City (Mexico)**
63. **Monte Carlo**
64. **Monterey (California)**
65. **Moscow (Russia)**
66. **Mount Everest (Nepal)**
67. **Mount Fiji (Japan)**
68. **Mount Kilimanjaro (Tanzania)**
69. **Napa Valley (California)**
70. **Naples (Italy)**
71. **Nashville (Tennessee)**
72. **Nazareth (Israel)**
73. **Niagara Falls (New York)**
74. **The Panama Canal (Panama)**
75. **Penny Lane (London)**
76. **Phnom Penh (Cambodia)**
77. **Purgatory**
78. **The Pyramids (Egypt)**
79. **Reno (Nevada)**
80. **Reykjavik (Iceland)**
81. **Rio de Janeiro (Brazil)**

82. **Rodeo Drive (Beverly Hills)**
83. **Rome (Italy)**
84. **Roswell (New Mexico)**
85. **Salem (Massachusetts)**
86. **Santa Fe (New Mexico)**
87. **Stockholm (Sweden)**
88. **Stonehenge (England)**
89. **The Taj Mahal (India)**
90. **Telluride (Colorado)**
91. **Tijuana (Mexico)**
92. **Tokyo (Japan)**
93. **The Vatican (Italy)**
94. **Venice (Italy)**
95. **Victoria Falls (Zimbabwe)**
96. **Waikiki (Hawaii)**
97. **Wall Street (New York)**
98. **Washington D.C.**
99. **Windsor Castle (London)**
100. **Yellowstone National Park (Wyoming)**
101. **Zurich (Switzerland)**

**GIVE ME LIBERTY OR AT LEAST A SONG SO I CAN SING ABOUT IT**

An event can either be something that has happened in your life, the life of someone you know or a historical event. It could even be something you make up.

Maybe you think of an idea for a song about two seasoned fighters who staged a bare-knuckle boxing event during the 1800s and fought round after round in a courageous showdown.

Of course, there are millions of events that have actually occurred over the last few thousand years you could also write about. And just because someone has already written about that event doesn't mean you can't do the same, perhaps from a different perspective.

Many of these categories will be crossover ideas, but that doesn't matter. For example, *"Hurricane"* by Dylan could either be a song about the person (Rubin Carter) or the event (a innocent man put into prison). And we won't go into the poetic license Dylan took with his story, but it proves the point that even historical songs can also be personal.

Here are a few examples of songs that have been written about historical events.

*"Children's Crusade"* by Sting
*"We Didn't Start the Fire"* by Billy Joel
*"Rock the Casbah"* by the Clash
*"Ohio"* by Crosby, Stills, Nash and Young
*"Battle of New Orleans"* by Lonnie Donegan

**101 Historical Events You Can Write A Song About**
1. Ray Kroc opens first McDonalds. (1954)
2. Anne Frank received a diary for her birthday. (1942)
3. Alexander Graham Bell initiates the first telephone call. (1876)
4. Gottlieb Daimler invents first gas-engineered motorcycle. (1885)
5. The first Olympics are held in Athens, Greece. (1896)
6. The Battle of Waterloo -- Napoleon's final defeat. (1813)

7. Spanish Inquisition introduced to uncover heresy. (1480)
8. The Hindenburg tragedy at Lakehurst, New Jersey. (1937)
9. Martin Luther publishes 95 objections to Catholic practices. (1517)
10. Custer's last stand at Little Big Horn. (1876)
11. Levi Strauss and Jacob Davis file patent for riveting men's work pants -- the first jeans. (1873)
12. J. P. Knight invents the traffic light. (1868)
13. First car radio is made is U.S. (1922)
14. Thirteenth Amendment to US Constitution outlaws slavery. (1865)
15. The Chicago Black Sox baseball scandal. (1919)
16. Joan of Arc is burnt at the stake by the English. (1431)
17. The Cuban missile crisis. (1962)
18. The Mai Li massacre. (1968)
19. Attila the Hun attacks western Europe. (445)
20. U.S. drops atomic bomb on Hiroshima, Japan. (1945)
21. "I Love Lucy" premieres on CBS. (1951)
22. Hitler becomes fuehrer of Germany. (1934)
23. Howard Carter discovers tomb of King Tut. (1922)
24. The British Perforated Paper Company invents a form of toilet paper. (1880)
25. U.S. Air Force pilot Chuck Yeager becomes first person to break the sound barrier. (1947)
26. Benjamin Franklin flies a kite in a thunderstorm. (1752)
27. The U. S. stock market crashes. (1949)
28. Neil Armstrong becomes first man to walk on the moon. (1969)
29. The death of Elvis. (1977)
30. Mary Phelps Jacob invents the bra. (1913)
31. The first Thanksgiving is held at Plymouth Plantation in Massachusetts. (1620)
32. John Lennon of the Beatles shot dead in New York City. (1980)
33. Albert Einstein publishes the Theory of Relativity and makes famous the equation $E = mc2$. (1905)
34. Timothy McVeigh, the 1995 Oklahoma City bomber, was executed. (2001)

35. San Francisco struck by earthquake. (1906)
36. Nuclear power disaster at Chernobyl in Ukraine. (1986)
37. Patricia Hearst, 19-year-old daughter of publisher Randolph Hearst, kidnapped by Symbionese Liberation Army. (1974)
38. The Transcontinental Railroad is finished. (1869)
39. More than 120,000 Japanese and persons of Japanese ancestry living in western U.S. moved to "relocation centers". (1942)
40. The battle of the Alamo in San Antonio, Texas. (1836)
41. John Pemberton Invents Coca Cola. (1886)
42. Prohibition begins in United States. (1920)
43. The Baseball Hall of Fame opened to the public in Cooperstown, New York. (1939)
44. Three civil rights workers murdered in Mississippi. (1964)
45. Walt Disney is born. (1901)
46. Dylan goes electric at the Newport Folk Festival. (1965)
47. The first canned beer is manufactured. (1935)
48. Life Savers candy developed by Clarence Crane. (1912)
49. The 40-hour work week goes into effect. (1940)
50. The battle of Gettysburg. (1863)
51. Nixon resigns after Watergate scandal. (1974)
52. Eleven ships land their 'cargo' of around 780 British convicts at Botany Bay in New South Wales. (1788)
53. Thomas Edison invents the phonograph. (1877)
54. The White House burns during the War of 1812.
55. Michelangelo begins painting the Sistine Chapel. (1508)
56. The Beatles' first appearance on the Ed Sullivan show. (1964)
57. George Washington is elected first president of the United States. (1789)
58. German Karl Benz is first to sell motor cars. (1885)
59. The Simpsons becomes the longest-running prime-time animated show. (1997)
60. Orson Welles' "War of the Worlds" is broadcast. (1938)
61. Terrorist explosion kills 237 U.S. Marines in Beirut. (1983)
62. The tin can is invented. (1810)

63. Thousands die in the Galveston hurricane. (1900)
64. The first 3-D movie is released. (1932)
65. Dr. Richard Gatling patents the first machine gun. (1862)
66. The Titanic sinks after hitting an ice berg. (1912)
67. Gandhi assassinated. (1948)
68. W. L. Judson invents the zipper. (1893)
69. Panama Canal opens. (1914)
70. The end of World War II. (1945)
71. Annie Edson Taylor becomes first person to ride down Niagara Falls in a barrel. (1901)
72. Polygraph machine invented by James Mackenzie. (1902)
73. The Green Bay Packers defeat the Kansas City Chiefs in the first Super Bowl. (1967)
74. Edwin Prescott patents the roller coaster. (1898)
75. John Sutter discovers gold in California. (1859)
76. Construction begins on the Great Wall of China. (14th century)
77. Japanese attack Pearl Harbor. (1941)
78. The Wright Brothers first flight. (1903)
79. Coffee first planted in Brazil by Europeans. (1727)
80. Meltdown at Three Mile Island. (1979)
81. Service of the Pony Express begins. (1860)
82. Clarence Birdseye invents frozen food. (1923)
83. Columbus makes landfall at what is now The Bahamas in the Americas. (1942)
84. Jim Jones's followers commit mass suicide in Jonestown, Guyana. (1978)
85. Sea battle between the Monitor and the Merrimack. (1862)
86. Martin Luther King, Jr. gives "I Have a Dream" speech. (1963)
87. Berlin Wall dismantled. (1989)
88. Charles Lindbergh flies across the Atlantic. (1927)
89. Jackie Robinson joins the Brooklyn Dodgers. (1947)
90. Almost $3 million stolen in the Brink's robbery in Boston. (1950)
91. Henry Ford installs first assembly line. (1913)
92. Samuel Colt invents the first revolver. (1836)
93. English fleet defeats Spanish Armada. (1588)

94. Marconi invents wireless telegraphy. (1895)
95. Yuri Gagarin becomes first man in space. (1961)
96. The death of Marilyn Monroe. (1962)
97. Color television introduced in U.S. (1951)
98. Bubble gum invented by Walter E. Diemer. (1928)
99. Leonardo da Vinci dies. (1517)
100. Instant coffee invented by George Washington. (1909)
101. Italian Galileo Galilei confirms that the sun is the centre of the universe. (1609)

**LIONS AND TIGERS AND BEARS, OH, MY!**

It's easy to imagine an animal inspiring a song and it's happened thousands of times. It might be a song about your dog who's been your best friend for life who is reaching old age. Or you might be inspired by an eagle soaring lazily against a blue sky.

Here are a few examples of songs written about members of the animal kingdom.

*"The Lion Sleeps Tonight"* by The Tokens
*"Elusive Butterfly"* by Bob Lind
*"Crocodile Rock"* by Elton John
*"The Chimpanzee Song"* by the Bare Naked Ladies
*"Horse With No Name"* by America

**101 Animals You Can Write A Song About**
1. **Chameleon**
2. **Dragonfly**
3. **Kangaroo**
4. **Warbler**
5. **Rattlesnake**
6. **Lovebird**
7. **Vulture**
8. **Bumblebee**
9. **Raccoon**
10. **Snake**
11. **Kingfisher**
12. **Salamander**
13. **Piranha**
14. **Starling**
15. **Parrot**
16. **Iguana**
17. **Mudskipper**
18. **Octopus**
19. **Panda**
20. **Persian Cat**
21. **Falcon**
22. **Swan**

23. **Rabbit**
24. **Wren**
25. **Viper**
26. **Meerkat**
27. **Eagle**
28. **Badger**
29. **Gorilla**
30. **Anaconda**
31. **Python**
32. **Black Widow**
33. **Greyhound**
34. **Chimpanzee**
35. **Mongoose**
36. **Bunny**
37. **Gnu**
38. **Wasp**
39. **Amphibian**
40. **Weasel**
41. **Tarantula**
42. **Boa Constrictor**
43. **Serpent**
44. **Jackrabbit**
45. **Sandpiper**
46. **Antelope**
47. **Hawk**
48. **Abyssinian Cat**
49. **Flicker**
50. **Bear**
51. **Bandicoot**
52. **Cockatoo**
53. **Cobra**
54. **Buffalo**
55. **Dolphin**
56. **Zebra**
57. **Ferret**
58. **Sparrow**
59. **Fawn**

60. **Hummingbird**
61. **Koala Bear**
62. **Monkey**
63. **Crab**
64. **Ptarmigan**
65. **Crocodile**
66. **Pelican**
67. **Chickadee**
68. **Woodpecker**
69. **Stork**
70. **Butterfly**
71. **Praying Mantis**
72. **Albatross**
73. **Tortoise**
74. **Armadillo**
75. **Ladybug**
76. **Canary**
77. **Skunk**
78. **Porcupine**
79. **Shark**
80. **Loon**
81. **Beetle**
82. **Crow**
83. **Chipmunk**
84. **Aardvark**
85. **Goose**
86. **Gecko**
87. **Toucan**
88. **Penguin**
89. **Scorpion**
90. **Toad**
91. **Moth**
92. **Beaver**
93. **Owl**
94. **Puppy**
95. **Fox**
96. **Gazelle**
97. **Gopher**

98. **Flamingo**
99. **Grasshopper**
100. **Anteater**
101. **Angelfish**

## PLANES, TRAINS AND AUTOMOBILES

There have been more than a few songs inspired by modes of transportation. Maybe it's a passing reference or maybe it's in the title of your song, but whether it's a song about driving across the country in your Chevy Nova or watching a freight train chug slowly along next to the highway, they always seem to evoke enough inspiration for a song or two.

Here are a few examples of songs written about various forms of transportation.

*"Big Yellow Taxi"* by Joni Mitchell
*"Bicycle Race"* by Queen.
*"Leavin' On A Jet Plane"* by Peter, Paul and Mary
*"Baby You Can Drive My Car"* by the Beatles
*"Little Red Corvette"* by Prince

### 101 Vehicles or Modes of Transportation You Can Write A Song About

1. **Limousine**
2. **Viking Ship**
3. **Dinghy**
4. **Jumbo Jet**
5. **Blimp**
6. **Mule Train**
7. **Dodge Charger**
8. **Battleship**
9. **Ferry**
10. **Cadillac**
11. **Yacht**
12. **Fire Truck**
13. **Truck**
14. **Glider**
15. **Vespa**
16. **Raft**
17. **Rowboat**
18. **Wagon Train**
19. **Street Car**

20. **Riverboat**
21. **Houseboat**
22. **Ocean Liner**
23. **Automobile**
24. **Airplane**
25. **Roller Skates**
26. **Stanley Steamer**
27. **Ferrari**
28. **Kayak**
29. **Submarine**
30. **Thunderbird**
31. **Maseratti**
32. **Catamaran**
33. **Stagecoach**
34. **Tractor**
35. **Jaguar**
36. **Dirigible**
37. **Covered Wagon**
38. **Sampan**
39. **Chevy**
40. **Zeppelin**
41. **Sloop**
42. **Ice Cream Truck**
43. **Ambulance**
44. **Boat**
45. **Tank**
46. **Ford**
47. **Taxi Cab**
48. **Harley**
49. **Learjet**
50. **Car**
51. **Alfa Romeo**
52. **Locomotive**
53. **Space Shuttle**
54. **Roller Coaster**
55. **Paddle Boat**
56. **Armored Car**

57. **Barge**
58. **Junk**
59. **Trolley Car**
60. **Stealth Bomber**
61. **Soap Box Racers**
62. **Camaro**
63. **Conestoga**
64. **Lifeboat**
65. **Jalopy**
66. **Motorcycle**
67. **Cruise Ship**
68. **Tugboat**
69. **Lexus**
70. **Hot Rod**
71. **Gunship**
72. **Caboose**
73. **Bicycle**
74. **Lamborghini**
75. **Sailboat**
76. **Baby Buggy**
77. **Canoe**
78. **Tricycle**
79. **VW Bug**
80. **Dog Sled**
81. **Bumper Cars**
82. **Porsche**
83. **Scooter**
84. **Bus**
85. **Jeep**
86. **Hovercraft**
87. **Gondola**
88. **Hummer**
89. **Mustang**
90. **Hydrofoil**
91. **Ox Cart**
92. **Skateboard**
93. **Airliner**
94. **Sled**

95. **Corvette**
96. **Schooner**
97. **Train**
98. **Hot Air Balloon**
99. **Biplane**
100. **Helicopter**
101. **Model T**

## MOTHER EARTH (FOR WHAT IT'S WORTH)

Perhaps nothing can inspire us more than Mother Nature. Whether it's the simple beauty of a evening sunset, a glittering rainbow after a morning rain or a grove of whispering aspens, they each have their own magic. And it seems as if the muse drifts a little closer at those times than others, so why not take advantage of it.

Here's a few songs inspired by Mother Nature.

*"Blue Bayou"* by Linda Ronstadt
*"A Good Year For The Roses"* by Elvis Costello
*"Islands In The Stream"* by Dolly Parton and Kenny Rogers
*"Ebony and Ivory"* by Paul McCartney and Stevie Wonder
*"Heart of Gold"* by Neil Young

## 101 Things Found in Nature You Can Write A Song About

1. **Sandstone**
2. **Granite**
3. **Lava**
4. **Quartz**
5. **Diamond**
6. **Ruby**
7. **Emerald**
8. **Amethyst**
9. **Crystal**
10. **Stone**
11. **Rock**
12. **Marble**
13. **Obsidian**
14. **Mica**
15. **Gold**
16. **Fool's Gold**
17. **Silver**
18. **Iron**
19. **Pearl**
20. **Ruby**
21. **Sapphire**

22. **Topaz**
23. **Turquoise**
24. **Jade**
25. **Bamboo**
26. **Bonsai**
27. **Pistachio**
28. **Hackberry**
29. **Strawberry**
30. **Huckleberry**
31. **Cherry**
32. **Cinnamon**
33. **Hickory**
34. **Mahogany**
35. **Nutmeg**
36. **Weeping Willow**
37. **Joshua Tree**
38. **Coconut Palm**
39. **Juniper**
40. **Pinyon**
41. **Blueberry**
42. **Honeysuckle**
43. **Clover**
44. **Sage**
45. **Mistletoe**
46. **Thyme**
47. **Coal**
48. **Flint**
49. **Copper**
50. **Magnesium**
51. **Graphite**
52. **Aspen**
53. **Cottonwood**
54. **Driftwood**
55. **Dandelion**
56. **Bouquet**
57. **Carnation**
58. **Corsage**

59. **Seeds**
60. **Blossom**
61. **Acorn**
62. **Cactus**
63. **Thorn**
64. **Grove**
65. **Orchard**
66. **Cypress**
67. **Laurel**
68. **Lily**
69. **Narcissus**
70. **Oak**
71. **Vine**
72. **Thistle**
73. **Shamrock**
74. **Cedar**
75. **Holly**
76. **Ivy**
77. **Orchid**
78. **Forget-Me-Not**
79. **Pine**
80. **Apple Blossom**
81. **Redwood**
82. **Poppy**
83. **Blue Spruce**
84. **Columbine**
85. **Mountain Laurel**
86. **Peach Blossom**
87. **Tulip**
88. **Sunflower**
89. **Goldenrod**
90. **Magnolia**
91. **Dogwood**
92. **Birch**
93. **Yucca**
94. **Maple**
95. **Jasmine**
96. **Pecan**

97. **Tiger Lily**
98. **Morning Glory**
99. **Lavender**
100. **Belladonna**
101. **Peyote**

## DO ANDROIDS DREAM OF ELECTRIC SHEEP?

I don't think I've ever come across a book title more intriguing than the one above. It is one of those type of lines that songwriters die for.

The line not only conveys a sense of wonderment, but words like "android", "dream" and "electric" are among those words I refer to as "power" words. Power words are usually nouns although in the example above dream is used as a verb and electric as an adjective. The interesting part of the theory here is that both words are also nouns when used in a different sense.

Oh, for the record, "Do Androids Dream of Electric Sheep?" is a science fiction novel by Philip K. Dick and is considered a classic. It was the basis for the movie "Blade Runner" although many liberties were taken with the story. Read it if you get a chance.

Nothing can inspire music quite like the mystery and romance of the heavens and the millions of stars glittering above. Maybe it's the emptiness we feel or the beauty of the moment, but the heavens are a wonderful source of inspiration. There is also a certain poetry in the names of stars and planets that beg to be used in song. The same thing goes for the world of fantasy with its myriad of people and beasts and the magical arts.

Here are a few examples.

*"Bad Moon Risin'"* by Creedence Clearwater Revival
*"Life On Mars"* by David Bowie
*"Blue Moon"* by The Marcels
*"Rocket Man"* by Elton John
*"Catch A Falling Star"* by Perry Como

## 101 Space, Science Fiction and Fantasy Ideas You Can Write A Song About

1. **Flash Gordon**
2. **Jaba the Hutt**
3. **Dragon**
4. **Rocket**
5. **Asteroid**

6. **Sword and Shield**
7. **Magic**
8. **Black Hole**
9. **Mermaid**
10. **Comet**
11. **Light Saber**
12. **Banshee**
13. **Voodoo**
14. **Seven of Nine**
15. **Terra**
16. **Warlock**
17. **Stargazing**
18. **Alpha Centauri**
19. **Galaxy**
20. **Troll**
21. **Zombie**
22. **Middle Earth**
23. **Wraith**
24. **Ice Caps of Mars**
25. **Castle**
26. **Sunspots**
27. **Gnomes**
28. **Enchantment**
29. **Orion's Belt**
30. **Flying Saucer**
31. **Hyper Drive**
32. **Little Green Men**
33. **Labyrinth**
34. **Klaatu Barada Nikto**
35. **Mothership**
36. **Goblins**
37. **Meteors and Meteorites**
38. **Ursa Major**
39. **Hellhound**
40. **Pixie**
41. **Faeries**
42. **Hex**

43. **Binary Stars**
44. **Faster Than Light**
45. **Cassini's Division**
46. **Dungeon**
47. **Robot**
48. **Big Bang Theory**
49. **Pegasus**
50. **Space Station**
51. **Knight**
52. **Tenth Planet**
53. **Lunar Eclipse**
54. **Milky Way**
55. **Death Star**
56. **Sorcery**
57. **Solar Flare**
58. **Callisto**
59. **Crystal Ball**
60. **Spell**
61. **Warp Factor Ten**
62. **Air Lock**
63. **Dark Matter**
64. **Io, Europa, Callisto and Ganymede**
65. **Constellation**
66. **Fortune Teller**
67. **Teleportation**
68. **Telescope**
69. **Ghost**
70. **Wizard**
71. **Trekkie**
72. **Men From Mars**
73. **Android**
74. **Capricorn**
75. **Elf**
76. **Area 51**
77. **Beam Me Up**
78. **Three Moons of Pluto**
79. **Little Dipper**
80. **Rings of Saturn**

81. **Venus**
82. **Merlin**
83. **Hubble's Law**
84. **Doppelganger**
85. **Perseids and Leonids**
86. **Solar System**
87. **Andromeda**
88. **Celestial Body**
89. **Ogre**
90. **Magellanic Cloud**
91. **Nymph**
92. **Orbit**
93. **Universe**
94. **Roswell**
95. **Hyperspace**
96. **Unicorn**
97. **Nova**
98. **Aphelion and Perihelion**
99. **North Star**
100. **Witch**
101. **Solar Nebula**

## SONGWRITERS TO LISTEN TO FOR INSPIRATION

What can better inspire songwriting than good music. I know there are those out there who refuse to listen to music while they are in the creative process, but you should listen to music constantly. It is like homework for songwriters.

And listen to a variety of music, not simply the stuff you enjoy. If you listen enough you'll realize there's good music everywhere, even in genres you don't usually listen to. There are great country songs and great heavy metals songs and, yes, even some pretty good rap music.

Now there are those of us that are sometimes in the creative mode and sometimes are not. There are others who seem to be in a creative state of mind most of the time. Of course, the other 99% of us envy them.

For the rest of us it's sort of like the in/out basket on an office desk. For awhile the in box fills up, but then we get energetic and the out box serves it's purpose. A friend of mine once described it as intake and output and basically believed you were either in one mode or the other, but whichever mode you find yourself in, take advantage of it.

If you are in output mode, enjoy that creative process and the new songs it brings. If you're in intake mode, use the time to listen to music, read books or whatever else stimulates you until the tray is full and you're ready to write again.

In our "songwriters to listen to for inspiration" we've listed what we believe are some of the finest songwriters of the last 50 years. The list is probably tilted to reflect our era of growing up, but the bottom line is, these songwriters deserve a special place in any CD or MP3 collection regardless of your musical preference. In addition to listening to them for inspiration, you should learn from them as well. (Please note that these songwriters are listed in no particular order.)

## 101 Songwriters You Should Listen for Inspiration
1. **Bob Dylan**
2. **Paul Simon (Simon and Garfunkel)**
3. **Lennon and McCartney (The Beatles)**

4. Eric Clapton (The Yardbirds/John Mayall and the Bluesbreakers/Cream)
5. Stephen Stills (Buffalo Springfield/Crosby, Stills, Nash and Young)
6. Shawn Colvin
7. Harry Chapin
8. Hank Williams
9. Randy Newman
10. Carole King
11. Mick Jagger and Keith Richards (The Rolling Stones)
12. Tom Paxton
13. Joni Mitchell
14. Sheryl Crow
15. Elton John and Bernie Taupin
16. Prince
17. Bob Marley
18. Jerry Garcia/Robbie Hunter/Bob Weir (The Grateful Dead)
19. John Fogarty (Creedence Clearwater Revival)
20. Don McLean
21. Johnny Cash
22. Ani DiFranco
23. Kris Kristofferson
24. Billy Joel
25. Chris Isaak
26. Sting
27. Jimmy Buffet
28. Don Henley/Glenn Frey/Joe Walsh (The Eagles)
29. John Sebastian (The Lovin' Spoonful)
30. Jimi Hendrix
31. David Wilcox
32. Willie Nelson
33. Joan Baez
34. Bruce Springsteen
35. Loudon Wainwright III
36. Dolly Parton

37. **Brian Wilson (The Beach Boys)**
38. **Leonard Cohen**
39. **John Prine**
40. **Neil Young (Buffalo Springfield/Crosby, Stills, Nash and Young)**
41. **Keb Mo**
42. **Tom Waits**
43. **James Taylor**
44. **Jack Johnson**
45. **Pete Townshend (The Who)**
46. **Phil Collins**
47. **Ray Davies (The Kinks)**
48. **Donovan**
49. **Kate Bush**
50. **Van Morrison**
51. **Carly Simon**
52. **Neil Diamond**
53. **Phil Ochs**
54. **Jim Croce**
55. **John Denver**
56. **Ian Tyson**
57. **Stevie Wonder**
58. **Roger Miller**
59. **John Mellencamp**
60. **Elvis Costello**
61. **Warren Zevon**
62. **Stevie Nicks (Fleetwood Mac)**
63. **Mark Knopfler (Dire Straits)**
64. **Frank Zappa**
65. **Dave Matthews**
66. **Otis Redding**
67. **David Byrne (Talking Heads)**
68. **Bonnie Raitt**
69. **Ricky Nelson**
70. **Nilsson**
71. **Bob Lind**
72. **Rod Stewart**
73. **The Brothers Gibb (The BeeGees)**

74. **Jimmy Webb**
75. **Robert Johnson**
76. **Gordon Lightfoot**
77. **Chuck Berry**
78. **Freddie Mercury (Queen)**
79. **Barry Manilow**
80. **David Bowie**
81. **Buddy Holly**
82. **Ian Anderson (Jethro Tull)**
83. **Cat Stevens**
84. **Roy Orbison**
85. **Jon Bon Jovi**
86. **Dan Fogelberg**
87. **James Brown**
88. **George Harrison (The Beatles)**
89. **Robbie Robertson (The Band)**
90. **Tom Petty (Tom Petty and the Heartbreakers)**
91. **Jackson Browne**
92. **Sly Stone**
93. **Kenny Rogers**
94. **Janis Ian**
95. **The Everly Brothers**
96. **Kurt Cobain (Nirvana)**
97. **Jerry Jeff Walker**
98. **Laura Nyro**
99. **Michael Jackson**
100. **Curtis Mayfield**
101. **Woody Guthrie**

## AN ALBUM/CD TO LISTEN TO FOR INSPIRATION

In November of 2003, Rolling Stone magazine released a special issue with what they considered the 500 Greatest Albums of All Time. The list was based on the votes of 273 rock musicians, critics and industry figures each of whom submitted a weighted list of 50 albums. Several music genres were featured in the list, including rock, blues, jazz, country western, hip hop and combinations thereof.

Since that time there has been much discussion regarding that list, but differences aside, the albums listed were no doubt some of the best music ever to grace our planet.

We've narrowed that list for our book and included mainly those albums which also contain songs by some of the best songwriters of our time. I'm sure your list would be much different. The purpose of listing these albums/CDs isn't an attempt to rate them as "our" top 101 albums of all time, but rather a musical collection that any songwriter would be proud to own and listen to for inspiration.

The purpose here is to not only listen to these songs so that perhaps the muse will flow more frequently, but to also listen to these masterpieces and determine why they are so good and why so many of the songs are classics. Listen to the words. What do they invoke in you? Listen to the melodies. What do they inspire?

### 101 Albums/CDs You Should Listen for Inspiration
1. **Sgt. Pepper's Lonely Hearts Club Band – The Beatles**
2. **Blonde on Blonde – Bob Dylan**
3. **Bookends – Simon and Garfunkel**
4. **Pet Sounds – The Beach Boys**
5. **Home Again – David Wilcox**
6. **Crosby, Stills and Nash – Crosby, Stills and Nash**
7. **Ladies of the Canyon – Joni Mitchell**
8. **Sail Away – Randy Newman**
9. **Sheryl Crow – Sheryl Crow**
10. **Centerfield – John Fogarty**
11. **Are You Experienced? – Jimi Hendrix**
12. **Cover Girl – Shawn Colvin**

13. **Live and Kickin' – Leon Redbone**
14. **The Kink Kronikles – The Kinks**
15. **Tim – The Replacements**
16. **Parallel Lines – Blondie**
17. **The Definitive Collection – Abba**
18. **Surrealistic Pillow – Jefferson Airplane**
19. **Santana – Santana**
20. **Pretenders – The Pretenders**
21. **The Dock of the Bay – Otis Redding**
22. **Heart Like A Wheel – Linda Ronstadt**
23. **Blue – Joni Mitchell**
24. **Rocks – Aerosmith**
25. **Dookie – Green Day**
26. **The Downward Spiral – Nine Inch Nails**
27. **Tea for the Tillerman – Cat Stevens**
28. **Ten – Pearl Jam**
29. **40 Greatest Hits – Hank Williams**
30. **If You Can Believe Your Ears and Eyes – The Mamas and The Papas**
31. **Remain in Light – The Talking Heads**
32. **Pearl – Janis Joplin**
33. **Stand! – Sly and the Family Stone**
34. **Sweetheart of the Rodeo – The Byrds**
35. **At Last – Etta James**
36. **In The Wee Small Hours – Frank Sinatra**
37. **Dusty in Memphis – Dusty Springfield**
38. **Lady Soul – Aretha Franklin**
39. **Appetite for Destruction – Guns n' Roses**
40. **Greatest Hits – Al Green**
41. **At The Filmore East – The Allman Brothers Band**
42. **A Love Supreme – John Coltrane**
43. **Legend – Bob Marley**
44. **Horses – Patti Smith**
45. **The Dark Side of the Moon – Pink Floyd**
46. **Tapestry – Carole King**
47. **Ramones – Ramones**
48. **Led Zeppelin – Led Zeppelin**

49. **Tommy – The Who**
50. **The Joshua Tree – U2**
51. **Rumors – Fleetwood Mac**
52. **Live at the Apollo – James Brown**
53. **Plastic Ono Band – John Lennon**
54. **The Great Twenty-Eight – Chuck Berry**
55. **Thriller – Michael Jackson**
56. **Astral Weeks – Van Morrison**
57. **Nevermind – Nirvana**
58. **Kind of Blue – Miles Davis**
59. **The Sun Sessions – Elvis Presley**
60. **London Calling – The Clash**
61. **Graceland – Paul Simon**
62. **Highway 61 Revisited – Bob Dylan**
63. **Revolver – The Beatles**
64. **What's Going On – Marvin Gaye**
65. **In Between Dreams – Jack Johnson**
66. **Songs in the Key of Life – Stevie Wonder**
67. **Every Picture Tells A Story – Rod Stewart**
68. **Green River – Creedence Clearwater Revival**
69. **Brothers In Arms – Dire Straits**
70. **Damn the Torpedoes – Tom Petty and the Heartbreakers**
71. **Music From Big Pink – The Band**
72. **Bluesbreakers – John Mayall with Eric Clapton**
73. **Live Dead – The Grateful Dead**
74. **Imperial Bedroom – Elvis Costello**
75. **Sweet Baby James – James Taylor**
76. **Aqua Lung – Jethro Tull**
77. **Hotel California – The Eagles**
78. **Do You Believe In Magic – The Lovin' Spoonful**
79. **The Heart of Saturday Night – Tom Waits**
80. **Lost Dogs and Mixed Blessings – John Prine**
81. **Forever Blue – Chris Isaak**
82. **Ghost In The Machine – The Police**
83. **A White Sport Coat and a Pink Crustacean – Jimmy Buffet**
84. **Purple Rain – Prince**

85. **The Complete Recordings – Robert Johnson**
86. **Keb' Mo' – Keb' Mo'**
87. **If You Could Read My Mind – Gordon Lightfoot**
88. **After the Gold Rush – Neil Young**
89. **Recent Songs – Leonard Cohen**
90. **Goodbye Yellow Brick Road – Elton John**
91. **Greetings from Asbury Park – Bruce Springsteen**
92. **52nd Street – Billy Joel**
93. **Nick of Time – Bonnie Raitt**
94. **Classic Hits – Jim Croce**
95. **Back Home Again – John Denver**
96. **The Neil Diamond Collection – Neil Diamond**
97. **At Folsom Prison – Johnny Cash**
98. **American Pie – Don McLean**
99. **Heads and Tales – Harry Chapin**
100. **Disraeli Gears – Cream**
101. **Angels Running – Patty Larkin**

## PLAY IT AGAIN, SAM

Watching a good movie can serve two purposes. First of all, it can serve as inspiration. And from inspiration flows the creative juices you require to create your next song. And secondly, sometimes you simply need a break. Watching a movie can free the mind and let you forget about songwriting for awhile. Sometimes each one of us needs to do that. It makes us better songwriters in the long run.

### 101 Movies You Can Watch to Inspire Your Next Song

1. *Forrest Gump* (1994)
2. *One Flew Over the Cuckoo's Nest* (1975)
3. *Chocolat* (2000)
4. *Mr. Smith Goes to Washington* (1939)
5. *My Fair Lady* (1964)
6. *The Shankshaw Redemption* (1994)
7. *When Harry Met Sally* (1989)
8. *From Here to Eternity* (1953)
9. *The Notebook* (2004)
10. *Sleepless In Seattle* (1993)
11. *For the Love of the Game* (1999)
12. *Dirty Dancing* (1987)
13. *Hero* (2004)
14. *Phenomenon* (1996)
15. *Gone With the Wind* (1939)
16. *Fantasia* (1940)
17. *Doctor Zhivago* (1965)
18. *Million Dollar Baby* (2004)
19. *The Sixth Sense* (1999)
20. *The Green Mile* (1999)
21. *It's A Wonderful Life* (1946)
22. *Titanic* (1997)
23. *The Night of the Living Dead* (1968)
24. *Moulin Rouge* (2001)
25. *The Sound of Music* (1965)
26. *Midnight Cowboy* (1969)
27. *High Noon* (1952)
28. *Fargo* (1996)

29. *Close Encounters of the Third Kind* (1977)
30. *Crossroads* (1986)
31. *The Wizard of Oz* (1939)
32. *Pay It Forward* (2000)
33. *Crash* (2004)
34. *Annie Hall* (1977)
35. *Casablanca* (1942)
36. *Frequency* (2000)
37. *Singin' In The Rain* (1952)
38. *The Patriot* (2000)
39. *Field of Dreams* (1989)
40. *Finding Nemo* (2003)
41. *What Dreams May Come* (1998)
42. *Kill Bill Vols. 1 and 2* (2003/2004)
43. *Raiders of the Lost Ark* (1981)
44. *The Godfather* (1972)
45. *Cold Mountain* (2003)
46. *Braveheart* (1995)
47. *Rudy* (1993)
48. *Powder* (1995)
49. *Stepmom* (1998)
50. *Armageddon* (1998)
51. *West Side Story* (1961)
52. *To Kill A Mockingbird* (1962)
53. *The Jazz Singer* (1927)
54. *The Postman* (1997)
55. *Independence Day* (1996)
56. *Life of Brian* (1979)
57. *Yankee Doodle Dandy* (1942)
58. *The Maltese Falcon* (1941)
59. *The Graduate* (1967)
60. *Star Wars* (1977)
61. *Philadelphia* (1993)
62. *G. I. Jane* (1997)
63. *Brian's Song* (1971)
64. *Psycho* (1960)
65. *Rocky* (1976)

66. *Some Like It Hot* (1959)
67. *Hope Floats* (1998)
68. *Rebel Without A Cause* (1955)
69. *Lawrence of Arabia* (1962)
70. *March of the Penguins* (2005)
71. *Erin Brockovich* (2000)
72. *Mutiny on the Bounty* (1935/1984)
73. *Goodfellas* (1990)
74. *Monsters Inc.* (2001)
75. *Duck Soup* (1933)
76. *Snow White and the Seven Dwarfs* (1937)
77. *Pretty Woman* (1990)
78. *Dave* (1993)
79. *The African Queen* (1951)
80. *Shane* (1953)
81. *The American President* (1995)
82. *Pulp Fiction* (1994)
83. *The Grapes of Wrath* (1940)
84. *50 First Dates* (2004)
85. *The Philadelphia Story* (1940)
86. *Coyote Ugly* (2000)
87. *The Wild Bunch* (1969)
88. *As Good As It Gets* (1987)
89. *Vertigo* (1958)
90. *The Scent of a Woman* (1992)
91. *The Birth of a Nation* (1915)
92. *Babe* (1995)
93. *Metropolis* (1927)
94. *Steel Magnolias* (1989)
95. *Mary Poppins* (1964)
96. *Annie* (1982)
97. *Joseph and the Amazing Technicolor Dreamcoat* (2002)
98. *Radio* (2003)
99. *Shrek* (2001)
100. *Chicago* (2002)
101. *Don't Look Back* (1967)

# RESOURCES

## BOOKS ON SONGWRITING

### Songwriting: Essential Guide to Rhyming: A Step-by-Step Guide to Better Rhyming and Lyrics
by Pat Pattison (Berklee Press Publications)

### How to Write Songs on Guitar: A Guitar-Playing and Songwriting Course
by Rikky Rooksby (Backbeat Books)

### Tunesmith: Inside the Art of Songwriting
by Jimmy Webb (Hyperion)

### The Craft and Business of Songwriting (2nd Edition)
by John Braheny (Writers Digest Books)

### 6 Steps to Songwriting Success
by Jason Blume (Billboard Books)

### Songwriters on Songwriting
by Paul Zollo (Da Capo Press)

### This Business of Songwriting
by Jason Blume (Billboard Books)

### Successful Lyric Writing
Sheila Davis (Writer's Digest Books)

### The Songwriters Journal: 52 Weeks of Songwriting Ideas and Inspiration
by Stan Swanson (Stony Meadow Publishing)

## RHYMING DICTIONARIES

### The Complete Rhyming Dictionary
by Clement Wood (Laurel)

### Essential Songwriter's Rhyming Dictionary
by Kevin M. Mitchell (Alfred Publishing Company)

### Oxford Rhyming Dictionary
by Clive Upton (Oxford University Press)

# RHYMING SOFTWARE

**Rhymesaurus (PurpleRoom.com)**
(Thesaurus and Rhyming Software)

**Rhyme Wizard (RhymeWizard.com)**
(Rhyming Software)

**McGill English Dictionary of Rhyme (BryantMcGill.com)**
(Rhyming Software)

**Rhymer (Rhymer.com)**
(Online Rhyming Dictionary/Rhyming Software)

**A Zillion Kajillion Rhymes**
(Eccentric Software)

# THESAURUS

**Webster's New World Thesaurus**
(Webster's New World)

**Roget A to Z** (by Robert L. Chapman)
(Collins)

# SOFTWARE

**Lyricist**
(Virtual Studio Systems)

**TrackNotes**
(Virtual Studio Systems)

**MasterWriter**
(MasterWriter.com)

**Garage Band**
(Apple)

**Finale Songwriter**
(Make Music)

**Band In A Box**
(PG Music)

# HARDWARE

**TASCAM MF-P01 4-Track Portastudio**
(Tascam)

**TASCAM Porta 02 MKII Portastudio**
(Tascam)

**Fostex MR-8 8-Track Digital Recorder**
(Fostex)

**Cakewalk SONAR Home Studio XL**
(Cakewalk Music Software)

**Omega Studio**
(Lexicon)

Printed in the United States
77936LV00004B/8

9 780978 792503